Buddy's Daughter in *Soulscape*

Buddy's Daughter
in
Soulscape

Story, Commentary, and Affirmation in a Life Well-Lived: Contemplative Prose Ending with Amen

Janis Constable

Foreword by Patricia Gale-MacDonald

RESOURCE *Publications* • Eugene, Oregon

BUDDY'S DAUGHTER IN *SOULSCAPE*
Story, Commentary, and Affirmation in a Life Well-Lived: Contemplative Prose Ending with Amen

Resource Publications
An Imprint of Wipf and Stock Publishers
199 W. 8th Ave., Suite 3
Eugene, OR 97401

www.wipfandstock.com

PAPERBACK ISBN: 979-8-3852-6294-6
HARDCOVER ISBN: 979-8-3852-6295-3
EBOOK ISBN: 979-8-3852-6296-0

VERSION NUMBER 04/23/26

Dedication

To my dad, Buddy,
with love and gratitude.

You shaped me—
body mind and spirit.
You mentored me
to become the fullest version of me—
to become most fully human.

With love and hugs, and really big squeezes,
from your little Jani
XOXOXO

OH DAUGHTER OF MINE . . ..

Oh daughter of mine
  may you grow, may you become—
    a river of life
      a light ever-glowing
        a love freely flowing.

May you approach all of life and living
  with kindness, with boldness, with wisdom.
    For aye, may you know the depth, the breadth and the reach
      of fullest, deepest, truest love.

May you know you are mine—
  you are precious, unique and beloved.
    I have held you and nurtured you and walked by your side.
      I have prayed for you.

As life moves us both onward, forward, into the Light, remember me.
  Remember my love.

Always and ever,
  remember my love.

Love, Dad
XOXO

CONTENTS

COMMENTARY

AFFIRMATION

CLOSING PRAYER

FOREWORD

"We shall not cease from exploration
And the end of all our exploring will be to arrive at where we started
And know the place for the first time."[1]

JANIS CONSTABLE HAS BEEN an explorer—a seeker—all of her life. From her roots in southern Ontario, through her early athletic endeavors and her later years as Emergency Room Nurse and Parish Nurse in Ministry, Janis' life has been a journey of self-discovery shaped by a hunger to know God in the mystery and the fullness of God's being. More recently, she has sought wisdom within the ancient teachings of Celtic spirituality.

Beginning in 2021, Janis published five books. In each one, the reader is invited into a contemplative experience of God that is mystical, luminous and profound. The filter and light of Celtic spirituality informs each of these books.

Buddy's Daughter in Soulscape is Janis' sixth book. Like her earlier books, the focus in this book is on the relationship between her personal experiences and her ever-evolving, ever-changing interior life—her soulscape as she calls it. As T. S. Eliot intimated in his poem, this journey of self-discovery most often begins when we leave home. But it is also true that at some point, inevitably, the spiritual journey will lead us back to our roots.

Buddy's Daughter is a story about going home—about Janis' decision to revisit her relationship with the one person who had the greatest

1. T.S. Eliot, "Little Gidding" in *Four Quartets*, 59.

influence on her life—her father. Written in three parts, the book begins with a memoir full of anecdotes that are warm and funny, as well as intense in their scope and depth. Story is followed by Commentary, where Janis reflects on the way Buddy's influence shaped her faith, her attitudes and her beliefs. She closes the book with a lyrical Affirmation of who and whose she is.

Buddy's Daughter is a celebration of family life. It is also a vulnerable, honest, sometimes raw account of the complexity of human relationships. It speaks of how love, perfect love, God's love, can be expressed through imperfect people. Buddy was a good man, but not a perfect man—a fact that Janis has the courage to make clear. Yet despite this or, perhaps, because of it, Janis' memories of her father are summed up by her four simple words *"My father was love."*

Buddy's unconditional acceptance and support prepared her for the challenges and joys of her adult life, and filled her life with light, vision and dreams. In revisiting their relationship through discernment and prayer, and then through her writing, Janis has been gifted with *"knowing the place, for the first time."* The place—her place as a beloved child held in God's love as expressed through Buddy's love—transforms her soulscape and frees her to journey into the mystery of what is yet to be.

Buddy's Daughter in Soulscape is an intensely personal account. At the same time, it is also an invitation to all of us to do as Janis did—to go home. We are invited to rediscover our own stories and, through reflection and prayer, to discern how our interior life has been shaped by our earliest relationships.

It is a courageous thing to choose to go home. There is risk in daring to revisit stories from our past. But the Celtic tradition teaches that it is precisely when we ground ourselves in our personal stories that our interior life, our soulscape, is freed to find itself once again, for the first time.

Reverend Patricia Gale-MacDonald
April 2025

PREFACE—WHAT'S IN A TITLE?

BUDDY WAS MY DAD. He had a formal given name, but he was nicknamed Buddy on the day he was born, and the name simply stuck. He was raised, up until age twenty, on a Maritime dairy farm. He served in the RCAF in World War II, and he settled in Toronto after the war. He soon married a city girl—a Toronto-born woman. In time they had two beautiful girls. I am their youngest daughter.

He attended night school in Toronto for many years, studying business, while working in various daytime jobs. His career work was principally in sales and in sales management, selling products in electronics, appliances, home interiors and carpets.

Buddy, my dad, worked hard all of his life. I learned later in my own life, about his early childhood years, and his youthful shenanigans. He was kind of a tough guy—a bit of a scrappin' bully—and a playful prankster. I think that his being in the Air Force—being subjected to their discipline and their regimented ways—was a highly formative time for my dad. He straightened out. Or, they straightened him out!

My dad taught me so very much. Much of my own personal formation, I credit to my father. He was organized, efficient, and timely. He was a good listener. I had to earn his trust, and I had to work hard to measure up to his tough standards. Nothing was ever handed to me. I had to earn it.

Little did I know in his strong, steadfast and ultra-strict ways, he was preparing me for a life in the real world—he was priming my personhood—he was coaching me for success in the working world. He was grooming Buddy's Daughter to be a go-getter, a goal-setter, an "I can" person, and a "get-the-big-picture" guru. He was showing me by his example, how to rise up "figuring it out," always moving forward with eternal optimism, and with an ever-conquering spirit. He asked me to dream big—to persevere—to never give up or quit—to never lower my standards. He taught me to always be aware of people, places, things—and time. Failure to do so, for sure, would result in missed opportunities, missed adventures, and misunderstandings. I am, truly, Buddy's Daughter.

In my teenage and young adult years, I was an athlete. Field Hockey and Synchronized Swimming (now renamed as Artistic Swimming) were my focuses—my heart and soul—my driven life—my dream life. Extreme fitness, think-on-your-feet-strategy, think-outside-the-box-choreographic-creativity, perfection-in-execution-of-high-degrees-of-difficulty, were simply matters of fact in my life, way back then. I can surely see my dad's powerful influence on my driven approach, in my sporting years.

I wrote some poetry, songs, and hymns, in my and thirties and forties. When Dad would read my works, he would hold the printed page up to his chest with both hands—up to his heart—and softly say these words to me "You have a gift, Jan. You truly have a gift. Never stop writing, and expressing yourself. Never stop sharing what's on your heart!"

After a thirty-three year career in Emergency Nursing, and ten years in Parish Nursing Ministry, I retired. And I've finally found the time to settle, into a deeply contemplative lifestyle. I've always been a contemplative soul, musing my way through issues—problems and scenarios—and through life itself.

Buddy's Daughter in Soulscape showcases my late career coming of wisdom—my intuitive knowing and my journey into self-knowing—which has been a soul-widening gift for me. This book beckons readers of all ages—it speaks to all those who are seeking 'to know themselves and see themselves' in the context of their own personal formation journeys. It begs to be read by you!

Writing is my newfound passion. It is an affirming journey! It allows me to gather, sort and clarify my thoughts and then share them widely with like-minded readers. All six of my published works are the literary fruits of my deeply contemplative sits. All of my writing is beautifully interlaced with the ancient Celtic Wisdom—which is truly, the golden thread and the very matrix of me. Sigh. . . . I wish my dad were still alive today, that he could take time—to read and to delight—in my works. Sigh again. . . .

The word, Soulscape, is poetically upheld in the dictionaries, as "the landscape of the soul." My soul—my interior life—is one lyrical landscape—my ever-morphing and ever-emerging Soulscape.

This collection of prose is written through the eyes of Buddy's Daughter—through my eyes. This curated selection of story, commentary and affirmation is an acknowledgment of a life well-lived—my life well-lived.

When and where my own contemplative thoughts echo those of the great poets, I reference them plainly. In so doing, I do not shamelessly elevate my prose to theirs. Rather, I hope to show that the depth of my contemplative thinking is actually shared thinking—shared wisdom—that is expressed broadly. Perhaps even universally, through all time. I hope to share truth and Light—and relevance—through my words.

As I have most surely evolved over time, so too my personhood and my approach—my whole self-image and my life-perspective—have evolved. I now know and understand myself. I now know and love myself. My affirmations will help you, the reader, to see the transformed, healed and whole, and self-aware Celtic Christian that I have become.

Come, enter into this narrative prose with a willingness to be called into your own contemplative depths—with an openness to respond in your own prayerful words—with a curiosity for life-learning. Come, let my uniquely odic soulscape form you and inform you, sculpt you and shape you. May my words poetify your own emerging soulscape. May this be so. Amen.

Janis Constable
April 2026

NOTE TO READER

You could read this book in the order as it is written, and see first-hand how *The Story* was foundational for *The Commentary*, and that both *The Story* and *The Commentary* gave rise to the powerful *Affirmations* of Buddy's Daughter.

Or, you can cut to the chase and go straight to the heart of the matter—to the colorful life-learning found in *The Affirmations*. You can then return to *Story* and *Commentary* after having been moved and stirred up and inspired by the pithy *Affirmations*.

However you read this book—in whichever order you choose to read this book—does not matter. What does matter is that you read with an open mind and an open heart, seeking to understand your very own soulscape.

Your book. Your choice. Your read. God bless you in your reading, in your understanding, in your own personal formation. Amen.

A NEW WORD

INLONRACANCE

Pronounced
in—LAHN—rahk—ahnse

Category
Noun

Origins

in	(interior)
lonrach	(Irish word for shimmer)
ance	(act of being, or process of being)

Meaning

1. An interior feeling of an all-encompassing joy arising within the self in response to a current life-circumstance, or personal circumstance. Simply, a joyful state of being, not outwardly expressed.
2. A sense of inner glow, or radiance, or shimmer caused by overwhelming joy in the moment.
3. That exquisite human interior experience of joy, as a shimmering light arising within.

Whereas *exuberance* is an external expression of joy arising, *inlonracance* is an internal shimmer of joy arising, which is delightfully suffusive and personal.

The Irish word for shimmer is lonrach (LAHN-rahk). Add a prefix of "in" to make it inner, inward or interior. Add a suffix of "ance" to make it "the act of"' or "the process of."

See also inlonracancy (noun)
inlonracant(adjective)

AUTHOR'S NOTE

EVER HAD THE FEELING that you were glowing from within—that you were so blessed, so overjoyed, so radiantly and exquisitely happy—but you had no word, no single word, to describe your interior exuberance and your volcano of erupting joy? Your perfect inner shimmer moment?

Well, that is me, right here, right now! I'm inwardly shimmering with joy! So, what is stopping me from making up a word that means exactly what I'm feeling? Nothing is stopping me!

Drumroll, please! My hot-off-the-press, newly-minted pseudo-portmanteau is *inlonracance*!

I am in complete, full-blown inlonracance, for only me to sense, for only me to experience. In this moment, I am all lit up in my own glowing, in my own inlonracance. Sigh. Wow!

Have you known inlonracance? Have you felt it? Have you cherished the moment? What do you call your inner joyful shimmering? Say it! Use the word! Appreciate its depth and texture and color! And its internal densities, translucencies and dimensions!

Inlonracance!

ACKNOWLEDGMENTS

I'D LIKE TO TAKE the time here to mention a few folks who have been so very valuable to me in moving forward with the publishing of *Buddy's Daughter in Soulscape*—those folks who have helped me to answer the question "To publish or not to publish?"

First of all, I'd like to thank the team at Wipf and Stock Publishing for believing in me, and for early on, seeing the merit of this work and its potentials in my named target audience. The publishing experience has been so very straightforward, thanks to the diligence of this team.

And my humble heart reaches out in gratitude to Reverend Patricia Gale-MacDonald, for writing such an insightful and evocative Foreword—for choosing to frame *Buddy's Daughter in Soulscape* within the powerful works, the treasured poetry, of T.S. Eliot. Her thoughtful words have most certainly elevated mine!

And, by extension, a humble thank you to both HarperCollins New York, and Faber and Faber U.K., for graciously granting permission for the use of the exquisite, Light-bearing T. S. Eliot quote.

And a big shout out goes to the endorsers—Merike Remmel, Tina Cabrio McDowell, and Reverend Deborah Hart—for taking their valuable time to read and review my unpublished manuscript, and then offer up their heartwarming praise. Each one of these special women has witnessed in real life, the emergence of a strong and able Buddy's Daughter over a fifty-year time-span, which has in turn enabled them to provide such glowing testaments—their seals of approval. Thank you, my friends!

And I cannot forget to mention my Beta readers, Rory MacDonald, Edite Sammons, Lesley Landry, Leslie Walker and Nancy Sawyers for opening my eyes to the real and raw reader-experience *of Buddy's Daughter in Soulscape.* Thanks for your honest and constructive criticism, and your encouragement. Your candor is most appreciated.

I would especially like to honor and give thanks in advance, for my readers. It's always your expressed joy in reading my words, and your new and emerging perspectives on relationships, life and living, that make my writing journey so very worthwhile.

I also wish to mention my newfound yet very dear friend, Barbara Brown. She is always interested—and interesting! She gives constant support and encouragement, and her authentic positivity and *joie de vivre* lead her—drive her—through all of her life and living. In fact her own colorfully engaging website tagline is "Be Interesting!" Barbara energizes and enlivens me in so many ways and I wish her every success in her own journey—into the writing and publishing world!

And I must give credit to my husband, Barry Constable, for always allowing me the time and the space to pursue my passions in writing, and for serving so very patiently as my go-to tech support. They say it takes a village, and he is a rock and a pillar in my village setting.

And last but in no way least, I offer my gratitude for God's ever-presence and provision. I have been blessed and gifted by God, and I have been loved and led by God throughout my writing journey. Thanks be to God.

STORY

BUDDY—THE FORMATIVE YEARS

My dad was a third generation Canadian,
born of parents of Scottish ancestry—
the Walkers and the Gourleys.

He grew up on a dairy farm, in rural Nova Scotia.
Up with the crows to do chores in the barn, then off to school,
then more barn chores after school,
followed by a family farmhouse supper
and homework by the light of an oil lamp.

Then off to bed early to do it all again the next day.

Weekends were different. There was no school.
So his own dad, Chester, always had special projects
saved up especially for the weekend,
to keep his two boys busy, and out of trouble.

Oil the combine. Clean out the shed.
Weed the pond. Restack the hay in the barn.
Paint the porch.
"Pick rock" on the north field.

Oh how my dad hated pickin' rock, in the summer heat
on the south-facing rolling slopes in the summer!
It was grueling hard and hot work—tough work—
and someone had to do it!

It was out there on the gentle rolling Nova Scotia hillside,
that many of my father's dream's were born,
in the monotony of manual labor,
out on the hillside dairy farm.

Sometimes on a Saturday morning,
after the morning barn chores were done,
and before his dad would assign any afternoon tasks,
my dad would collect his fishing gear
and head up and over the massive hill
(the family farm was aptly named Hillside Dairy Farm!)
to get to the shores of the
St Andrew's River.

This was his special place.
This was his special time to just be a boy, to be a kid,
a carefree kid who loved to fish, to dream—
dreaming of fishing from his own boat—
a wide-eyed kid with people smarts,
and mechanical smarts,
and hard-working smarts.

A child who loved his own life on the farm,
but who also knew there was a lot more "out there"
in the industrializing world.

A child who could see that with a little hard work,
one could have anything they wanted in the world.

Dad was only five years old when the Great Depression rolled in,
paralyzing the nation.
His recollections included always-feeling-hungry—
no more extras anymore,
or second helpings at dinner and supper,
and often with a motley crew
of transient hungry farmhands
joining them for a meal
or two or three
during the week.

He said though, there was always pie for dessert.
No matter what, his mom would make a pie everyday,
and in those days, if they were really lucky,
some homemade rolls and biscuits to fill up on.
He knew that other families
didn't have it as good—
they had only bread for supper,
and no pie.

In 1939, World War II broke out,
and my dad was still too young to enlist.
As soon as he could, he did.
He bought and packed a large trunk,
and packed it with his meager possessions.

He took the train to Toronto—
his first train ride ever—and his first trip away from home ever!
He got on an RCAF bus,
and he found himself bound for a whole new world,
stationed with the RCAF at Trenton Ontario,
and later on, at Clinton Ontario.

He worked on the mechanicals of the aircraft,
under the supervision of licensed mechanics.
He did drill. So much drill!
Lined up for inspection.
Played in-house basketball with the guys.
They ate in the noisy mess hall.

They got called in quite frequently to the Lieutenant's Office,
for reprimand,
be it for their shoddy, sloppy work in the hangars,
or for their silly shenanigans
and blatant social misconduct.
The boys were often just being boys!!!

He danced at dance hall dances
with a young WD, Irene,
who would one day become his beloved wife.
He learned to smoke—cigarettes and cigars—
everyone smoked, so he said.

When the war was finally over,
my dad rented a basement apartment in Hamilton,
from Mr and Mrs Walmersly.
In time, their daughter Shirley
and her boyfriend Harry,
and my dad's then girlfriend, Irene,
were an inseparable foursome.

Their friendship circle expanded
to include some colleagues from work—
the Bennett's and the Ball's, and the Collin's.

Eventually all of these young people were marrying, buying homes,
and starting families of their own.
Dad married mom in 1951,
and bought their first house in Burlington—
on the shores of Lake Ontario
in the quiet neighborhood of Roselawn,
in Old Port Nelson—
an idyllic start for family life,
in the fantastic fifties.

My sister and I came along in '56 and '57,
and my parents were overjoyed with their perfect wee family.

The scene is set. Buddy grew up on a farm.
He read the newspaper daily to become more worldly.
He was educated through the RCAF,
and at night school business school.

He was a self-taught handyman, learning many tricks of the trades,
  in plumbing, electricity, carpentry, HVAC, metalworking,
    and in gardening, along the way.

He loved getting his hands into the soil.
  It always reminded him of his farming roots—
    his hearty, hardy, handy,
      wholesome beginnings on the family farm.

He was a dreamer and he found ways to make most of his dreams come true.
  He set his sights on his goals, and he accomplished them all.
    He looked to the future with optimism and hope—always hope.

He was a good man.
  An all round great guy.
    And he was my dad. My daddy.
      And I am so proud to be Buddy's Daughter.

Blessed be the fathers.
  Blessed be the dads.
    Blessed be the daddies
      of all time—in all place—in all hearts. Amen.

MY FATHER WAS LOVE

I always knew I was loved.

Whether as a youngster
   when my dad was sitting beside me on the couch at home,
      with his big strong arm around me
         while singing Christmas Carols
            together on Christmas Eve,

OR, whether as a toddler
   walking with my daddy in the hardware store aisles,
      and I instinctively reached up to hold his big strong hand,

OR, at age 22,
   when I caught his proud smile from afar
      as I strode across the stage at Convocation Hall
         to receive my U of T degree . . .

I knew I was loved. I felt loved.
   My father, was love.

At times throughout my life, I witnessed—and experienced—
   the many colours of my dad's emotions.
      His anger, his disappointment, his hurting,
         his sadness, his loyalty, his understanding,
            his pride, his joy, his wisdom.

But, none of these were greater than, or bigger than,
more colorful than, or warmer than,
his love for me—his love for me and my sister.
We knew his love. We felt his love.
My father, was love.

When I moved away from Ontario to Newfoundland, at age 25,
my dad drove with me in my brand new car,
all the way from Toronto to the North Sydney ferry docks,
where he would bid farewell to me,
as I boarded the ferry to the far-off land—
The Rock.

He held me close in a hold-me-tight-never-let-me-go hug.
He didn't hold back his tears.

"His little girl"—I—was all grown up—
an independent, competent young woman,
with broad shoulders,
head set squarely on those capable shoulders.
He was missing me already.
His overflowing tears spoke volumes.
I knew his love. I felt his love.
My father, was love.

May we all be so privileged
to live in the wonder and in the shelter of our Father's Love.

May we honor this love.

May we even embody this love as our own,
that others may come to know the meaning
of unconditional love—
of their own father's formative love. Amen.

CHURCH IS A FAMILY AFFAIR

I grew up in Burlington, Ontario, Canada, in the fifties and sixties.
Our ranch-style bungalow
was at the end of a tar and gravel road,
right beside a large vegetable farm.

To get to school, we had to walk east,
and follow a footpath across that same farmfield.
Snowdrifts and springtime muck
made for fun walks to and from school!

To get to church, we would walk as a family to the west,
only a quarter mile, crossing a creek
on the large flat stepping stones.
Rain or snow, we'd all dress for the weather,
navigating the creek crossing together,
and go to church on Sunday mornings,
all year round.

My sister and I would go downstairs,
to Sunday School
while my parents went upstairs to the Sanctuary,
for Sunday Service.

There was never any question about going to church. We all just did.
I believe it was my dad's doing,
insisting on our regular attendance,
to create a sense of belonging.

And we all felt like we belonged—
in the community—in a church family—
to a faith community which was
steeped in tradition and mystery.

I believe my dad felt that there was more order in life—
a higher order—and a sense of family unity—
when we all began the week
together in church as a family.

He also truly loved our ritual Sunday Roast Dinners.
He had grown up on the farm with meat and potatoes,
so of course,
Sunday dinner was always a "roast something"
with gravy—Yum!

He was absent from a lot of weekday dinners
due to his ongoing night school commitments,
so he insisted on calling Sunday dinner, "Family Time."

I know that my dad truly appreciated
the church's help through Sunday School,
in fostering good moral teachings
and reinforcing the simpler rules of life—
like the Golden Rule—and Love Thy Neighbor.

The church inherently modeled four very special prayerful words—
Please, Thank You, I'm Sorry, and I Love You.

Dad wanted us kids to grow up in a church family,
feeling valued and connected,
feeling that we were indeed "part of",
and, knowing a strong sense of belonging.

Dad wanted his family to be nurtured by the church family.
It's what he grew up with in Nova Scotia,
and he dearly wanted this for his young family.

Week after week, I remember us all arriving at the church.
It was always a special time
at the oversized—giant—arched wooden church doors.
Everyone was so happy to see us,
and they all welcomed us warmly—
they reached out through the doors
to greet us with their love.

Smiles were everywhere. Jovial laughter echoed all around.
There was no pretense, or airs—no hobnobbing or schmoozing
with the who's who—no keeping up with the Joneses.

Just really nice neighbors
in a really nice quiet neighborhood,
being really, really nice to everyone.

It was a very wholesome bunch of neighbors
gathering—congregating—
to encourage each other, to support each other,
and to serve those who needed their help.
And, of course, to worship together.

My dad did his turns with his neighbors,
as a Greeter, as an Usher,
and, as an Offerings Steward.

After Service, us kids would always manage
to find our parents somewhere upstairs,
and we would all wait patiently in line with them,
to meet and greet the minister.

I distinctly remember experiencing first-hand,
the sheer contrast
of the solid, firm-grip handshake
from the minister's super-soft hand.
The skin of his hand was soooooo soft!
But not his grip!!!

My dad would often pass a tightly folded note to the minister
when he was shaking his hand after Service.
I later learned that these were hand-scribbled questions,
which my dad had written for the minister
during the Service.

It was my dad's way of feeling connected to his minister.
My dad never shied away from asking questions of anyone,
if he wanted to know an answer!

My memories from my childhood—of my church family—are golden.
And more than this, my memories of my father at the church,
are pure gold.

I loved him. Everyone loved him.
It felt good to be part of this special love.
I always felt so warm all over,
through and through.

And to this day, no matter to where my husband and I move,
we always look for a church where we feel
welcomed, nurtured, gathered in close—and loved.

I thank my dad for my church upbringing—
for my church family experience.
Today I have a strong sense of belonging,
through my own church family,
and, I treasure this.
I will always treasure this. Amen.

BUDDY—THE WONDER YEARS

My dad, Buddy, had a dream. It was a big dream.
He wanted to see all of North America, coast to coast to coast—
all provinces and states—
in one continuous camping road trip
with the whole family.

It would mean taking his girls out of school for a year or more,
and having all of the necessary funds saved up
in order to afford this incredible adventure.

In time, when he realized that this dream
was going to be financially next to impossible,
he then set his sight on camping in every campground
which was a reasonable
family-drivable-distance from home.

This meant throughout all of Ontario,
and in all of the Maritime provinces—
through all of the New England States—
and in any of the northeastern states
which bordered on the Great Lakes.
Now that, he felt was doable!

He would not get to see the Rocky Mountains
or the California Gold Coast in this downsized version.
And, he also wouldn't get to see
the infamous Route 66 or the Grand Canyon.

Disneyland and Disneyworld weren't high priorities for him,
so it was getting easier for him to frame his new vision—
his smaller and more realistic dream—
and make it a reality.

We camped together as a family for twelve consecutive summers,
in multiple provincial parks and state parks.
We stopped camping, the year we built the pool.
That was our new playground,
right in our own backyard!

We camped beside rivers, near thundering waterfalls,
ancient carved rock gorges, caves,
First Nations' Lands, ocean shorelines and tidal bores.

I remember playing and swimming in all kinds of waters—
New Hampshire golden sparkling shallow waters
with its soft sandy beaches,
Craigleith darkwater shale rock shorelines,
Wasaga freshwater surf waves,

"Temagami Blue" deep waters, chilly Oastler shores,
salty spray surfs at Fundy Bay Oceanside,
and the Black River
blackwater clam encrusted fastwaters,
where the cool shallow waters
were burnt orange in color,
because the water
had a very high iron content.

From each of the wonders at The Sault (Sault St Marie),
The Polar Express, Peggy's Cove, Smuggler's Notch,
Whiteface Mountain, Ausable Chasm,
Watkins Glen, and Frankenmuth,
we gazed, we gawked, we gasped—
we stood in awe
of all the natural landscapes.

Family camping trips were just idyllic.
Time meandered, and sometimes simply stood still.
Scenery spoke.
History sang out.
Ancient was palpable.
Friendly camper faces were everywhere.

There was always Mom's
Coleman-stove-cooked-meals shared at the picnic table
and great campfires in the early evening.
Toasted marshmallows were yummy.
We all slept very well every night,
in our sleeping bags, on air mattresses,
in our camper—our tent-trailer.

We were in the water everyday, except for rainy days,
and I don't really remember many of those.
I guess we played cards,
or Chinese checkers, or monopoly,
inside the tent on yucky weather days.

Sunburn and mosquito bites,
scraped knees and stubbed toes
were all a fact of life. No big deal.

My dad's dream was a beautiful dream.
He just wanted his family
to see as much of the world as was humanly possible, together.

He wanted his family holidays,
to be spent in interesting places that were new to us—
among interesting people who were new to us—
just spending time being interested and interesting,
all of us—all together.

So we didn't see the Rockies, or the Grand Canyon.
But we did see the Agawa!

We shared a wonderful bond through all of our camping days.
We were a close knit family with stories to tell,
adventures to recount and exaggerate—
and daily dreams lived out together.
We have a lifetime of memories
to hold onto—to share.

My dad's dream—
of seeing as much of North America as we could possibly see
through camping in the parks—
became our reality.

Dad didn't just talk about his dream—
he showed us.
And we all lived out his dream, together.

Those camping years were special—so very special—
they were our Wonder Years.

Might every family know the joys of living out their dreams—
be they small or grand.
May we all live out our dreams.

Thanks be to my dad,
for sharing his dream with us,
and then making the dream come true. Amen.

BUDDY—THE FUN-LOVIN' GUY!

Just a few vignettes, to paint a sweet picture of my fun-lovin' dad.

Church Capers

My neighbour in Burlington, Mr Stewart,
told me this story when I was nine years old.
My family was moving away from Burlington to Etobicoke,
and Mr Stewart was having fun,
recounting some exploits involving my dad.

"Hey Jani! You know that your dad and I
were partners as Offering Stewards at church, right?"
I nodded, and waited for a pun or a punch line.

"Well, do you know what he said to me one Sunday morning,
right before we would walk up the aisle, solemnly,
with the offering plates overloaded and overflowing?"
I gave him a quizzical look.

"Your dad whispered loudly in my ear
'DAH DAH-DAH-DAH!!! CHARGE!!!'

"It was all we could do to keep a straight face and walk a straight line,
and keep from bursting into tears and laughter!
I'll never forget your dad, and all of his fun!"

Green Pie Shenanigans

My sister's favourite pie, was "Green Pie."
A lime-flavoured creamy whipped delight
set in a chocolate cookie-crumbled pie shell.

My dad was in an ultra silly mood
when dessert was served one night, after dinner.

And to my mom's horror and disbelief
(she practiced perfect table manners at every meal),
my dad plunged his pointer finger
deeply into the mile high pie,
extracting it slowly with a large green wad.

He then stared me into a challenge!
I met the challenge
by sinking my whole small hand into my 3" high slice of pie.
We were ready. We were primed.
My mom actually yelled, "No! Bud! Don't!!!"

Too late!
His green-wadded pointer was already enroute to my nose,
and my pie-clad palm landed squarely
on both his nose and mouth.

What a moment! What a riot!
What sheer joy in having a green-pie-food-fight!
My mom lightened up and actually laughed with us—
when she saw the innocent fun.

Thanks Dad, for making fun memories—
for being the instigator—
for reminding us of the simple joys
of silly play and silly fun.

Speed Demons

I honestly believe that my dad invented the jet-ski,
long before the current manufacturers!!
My dad had an inborn need—
an unspoken and unfulfilled—need for speed.

He bought a seventeen-foot Tempest motor boat,
for our family's use on Lake Simcoe.
When we weren't around,
Dad would take the boat way way way out
into the middle of the lake.

With no other boats around, he'd drive it hard—drive it fast—
in tight figure eights and in circles, and doubling back and forth
over his own wakes repeatedly.
At breakneck speed.
It was his thrill. It was his *joie de vivre.*
It was his release.

One day, he took my sister out there with him.
She didn't have her car driver's license yet,
but she too discovered her inborn need for speed.

Well, when the two of them came home
and told us of their kamikaze feats,
we were all a little wide-eyed.
My fun lovin' dad and his frail, timid, unadventurous daughter
were bonding over their shared adrenaline-rush stories!

I wish my sis and my dad had lived long enough
to tryout their skills on the modern day jet-skis.
They would be in their glory.
They would be glowing in their own delight.
They would be energizing all of us
with their exuberance and joy!
They would ignite us all,
with their fire!

Bluebird of Happiness
My nana was a member of a church ladies' group "The Bluebirds."
My dad loved to tease and provoke
his prim and proper mother-in-law, my nana.

When he was sitting near her on the couch,
he'd intentionally lift his leg and let go a rumbling fart, or two.
My nana was mortified, and she'd blush deeply,
and say "Oh, Bud!" and turn away from him.

One May, she was shopping at Eaton's for his birthday card.
She saw the perfect card, and it truly made her blush!

Three times, she took it to the cashier,
changed her mind, and put it back in the rack.
She finally summoned her courage and bought it.
Then she had to muster her nerve to sign her name!

My dad's May 5th birthday came along,
and Nana joined us for supper and birthday cake.
Dad was barely finished his cake when she blurted out
"Better open this card now Bud, before I change my mind.
Before I lose my nerve!"

Well, those words got all of our attention! Dad opened the card.
The front of the oversized card had a picture
of a pretty, smiling bluebird in flight.
Rather innocuous, it seemed.
The text on the front of the card, read,
"*May the Bluebird of Happiness . . .* "

Turning the page, we saw a crazed, careening, cross-eyed, grimacing,
giant bluebird, with its wings erect over its head,
approaching to land on a candlelit birthday cake—
the flames were dramatically leaning
as with the incoming great gust of wind!

And the text continued . . .
"May the Bluebird of Happiness crap all over your birthday cake!!!"

My then ninety year old nana (she lived to be 101!) did it!
She got my dad back! Finally! Well done Nana!!!

Dad was speechless at first,
then he belly-laughed,
then he roared with tears a-flowing!
"You got me, Rose! You got me big time!
This card needs to be framed. It's a classic.
Ha! Ha! You did it! You got me !!!"

We were all speechless.
But, looking at my nana, we saw her sparkle!
Out from under her "prim and proper,"
her playful spirit had emerged
and it was soaring high with the rest of ours.

I'll never look at a bluebird in quite the same way, ever again!!!

May we all know what fun is.
May we all make our own fun along the way.
When life gets heavy, or dark, or just plain tough,
may we find a way to lighten up and brighten up,
and just have a little fun.

May we all know, that laughter can heal, that laughter can bond.
May our playful spirits
bring Light and laughter to those in need. Amen.

LOST IN ARROWHEAD

I was lost. But I wasn't afraid. I wasn't even worried.
My dad would find me. I knew my dad would find me.

I was five years old in the 1960's,
camping with my family at Arrowhead Provincial Park,
near Huntsville, Ontario, Canada.

My dad had dropped me off at a friend's campsite,
a few rows over from our own campsite.
He had said before he drove away,
"Now you remember Jani, how to get home?
Make sure you're home for lunch at noon."

I remember smiling and saying "Yes, Daddy,"
because I had walked that route quite a few times already,
during our three week family camping holiday adventure
at Arrowhead.
And I knew my way.
And Dad knew I knew my way.
I waved goodbye to my dad,
and watched him drive away.
It was around 10 AM.

I played with my little playmate for awhile,
and her mom eventually said
"You should be heading home now Jani.
Your mom will have your lunch ready for you soon."

So, I said goodbye, and I headed home—toward my family's campsite.
   I walked with confidence, knowing exactly where I was going,
      or so I thought.

In time, nothing looked familiar,
   and then I guessed that I had made a wrong turn somewhere.
      I decided to turn around
         and see if I could find where I went wrong—
            to see if I could find
               a more familiar camp road.

An older woman watched me as I doubled back a number of times,
   with me passing by her own campsite multiple times,
      on the camp road.
         She called out to me "Are you lost?"

I said convincingly, "No!"
   I think I was intentionally trying to convince myself
      that I wasn't lost,
         because "lost" was a really bad thing,
            according to my dad!

She started to worry about me, and shortly,
   she came over to meet me on the camp road.
      She asked me if I knew my campsite number.
         I said no,
            but I could describe our camper and our car
               in great detail!

She made me a ham sandwich, while she figured out what to do.

There were no cell phones,
   and no Emergency Alarms were installed in the park.
      Signage for the camping sections
         and campsites was limited.

I happily sat at the picnic table by myself.
I leisurely munched away on my sandwich,
and drank my tall glass of cold milk.
I was enjoying the nice lady's hospitality.

I wasn't upset. I wasn't worried. I wasn't scared.
I just knew that things would work out.
I trusted that my dad would know I was late
and that he would come looking for me—
and that he would find me.

My dad was my hero and I had every reason to believe in him—
to trust in him—to hope in him.

And, sure enough,
just as I was reaching for the homemade sugar cookies
that the lady had set out for me,
I saw my dad.

He was driving slowly—very slowly—
gazing left and right
into every campsite on both sides of the road,
hoping to catch a glimpse of his precious wee Jani.

He was driving his giant brown Buick Le Sabre.
He grinned ever so broadly the minute he saw me!!!
I jumped up from the picnic table and I ran toward him.
I don't even think I thanked the nice lady.
In the moment, that didn't matter.

My dad had driven around and around and around the park,
looking for me, and he found me!!!
I KNEW HE WOULD FIND ME
BECAUSE MY DAD
WAS SIMPLY THE BEST DAD EVER!!!

He could do anything! He built things. He fixed broken things.
He made things grow
in our vegetable garden and flower gardens.
He knew what was/wasn't a weed.
He knew how to replace dead sod.
He planted beautiful groves
of white birch trees
along the sides of our yard.

He poured a concrete patio,
and he was always leveling the patio-stone walkway.
He was a strong man. A determined man.
A smart man. A good man.
HE COULD DO ANYTHING!
He was my protector and my guide.
He was my hero.
Of course, he could find me!

In looking back into my memory of this story,
I ask myself over and over and over again
"Why was I so calm? Why was I so optimistic and confident?
Why was I not afraid?"

And I think that it's because at a very early age,
my dad had instilled confidence in me.
Through his own natural confidence,
I easily embodied it.

He not only showed me confidence,
he taught me about confidence!
He did say to me once
when I was still pretty young, that
'Bravery—confidence—is in you,
like it is in the lion.
But you have to know this.'

And my dad probably knew Thoreau's famous words too.
  "Go *confidently* in the direction of your dreams."[1]
    I'm sure he quoted these exact words to me, once upon a time.

Dad was a great role model,
  even though at that young age,
    I didn't have a clue what a role model even was.
      But he was just that.
        And obviously a really good one!

He taught me to think through a problem—
  to always approach things slowly—
    to take time to think things through.
      Figure it out. If something "was missing,"
        go back to "the known," and fill in the blanks.

He taught me that there's an answer to every question,
  and a solution for every problem.

He also taught me to trust—
  to trust in myself and to trust in him.

These are all life-lessons which over the years,
  have shaped me—and shaped my life—in a really good way.

I am grateful to my dad
  for his teachings, his shared wisdom, his personal example—
    and his love—his fatherly love.
      I am strong. I am brave.
        I know my way. I'll find my way.
          I am not lost. I am found. Amen.

1. Paraphrase of Henry David Thoreau, in *Walden*, 241.

"SOMEDAY WHEN YOU'RE OLD ENOUGH . . . "

When I asked questions like
"If everybody loved JFK so much, why did they shoot him?"
or, "Why does a mommy doggie have eight puppies
at a time, and a lady mommy
only have one at a time? Doesn't that hurt?"

or, "Why do ladies wear hats in church, and not the men?"
or the one that made my dad blush beet red
and squirm in his chair
"Dad, What's a virgin?
Why was Mary so special?
Why does God not favour me
the way He favoured Mary?"

In my childhood, certain subjects were like a no-fly-zone.
Don't go there. At all cost, don't go there!
The parents knew this, but us kids did not.
We had no clue! We were just inquisitive kids!

So, every once in awhile, we'd unknowingly ask a zinger
in the banned subjects of religion, violence, and sexuality,
and, we were calmly met
with my parents' schooled response
"Someday when you're old enough,
I'll tell you."

I believe my dad was doing his very best to let us be children,
for as long as we could be.

He didn't want us growing up too soon,
or finding out about the unfairness
and injustices and violence in the world.
In his eyes, some secrets, some mysteries,
were better kept as secrets and mysteries—
sex talk and all.

I'm so grateful to my dad for protecting us
from some of the cold harsh realities of life.
Ours WAS an idyllic childhood—carefree—easy, breezy, and naïve.

And we respected our parents' withholding of, and deferring of,
answers until we were older.
We got to be kids, in a kid's world.
And, we grew up in time, at the right time,
and we found all the answers we needed,
along the way.

Thank you God, for parents,
and for their responsible and protective actions
where their children are concerned.

May we all be grateful for the care and concern of parents,
for their sheltering love, for their ever-reaching hope
and vision for all of humanity. Amen.

MAKING CHANGE—GETTING IT RIGHT

I was all of seven or eight years old,
when my dad decided to try and push me forward
in applied math skills.
He wanted to know if I could grasp the concept,
of making change.
And, he had a plan.

Dad invited me to kneel on the floor,
in front of our large circular marble coffee table,
in the living room.

He had already cleared away the large full color "coffee table books"
and the floral centerpiece.
He sat leaning forward, on a seafoam green cloth-covered chair,
on the other side of the low table,
when he beckoned me to kneel.

It was winter, and there was a crackling fire in the fireplace.
I had just come in from skating
on the nearby flooded rink on the farmer's field.
My feet were icy purply cold.

I remember my mom interrupting us,
to help me put on
some pink thick woolen socks.
She would then bring to me,
hot cocoa to warm me.

Dad reached into his pocket and pulled out a large handful of change.
He divided it randomly in half,
and gave one half to me on my side of the coffee table,
and he kept the other half on his side.

He said to me "I want to teach you to make change. It's not hard.
It's just about using what you already know in school—
about adding and subtracting—and applying it to the real world.
You always have to take what you learn in school,
and make it work for you in the real world."

He pushed a quarter toward me, and said "How much is this?"
I said "25 cents."

He took the quarter away,
and pushed two dimes and a nickel toward me,
and said "How much is this?"
I said "25 cents."

He said "Good. You can add."
He took away a dime, and said "How much is this?"
I said "15 cents."
He said "Great! Your subtracting is good too!"

He then put all of his coins to the side and said
"Listen carefully. I'm not trying to confuse you.
Put all of your money to the side,
but just keep one single quarter in front of you.
Right now, all you have to work with,
is one quarter, Okay?!"

I did what he said and I remember
twiddling the quarter between my fingers and thumb.
I looked at him for my next instruction.

He said, "Let's just say I have a chocolate bar right here,
and you want to buy it right now, and it costs 15 cents.
Can you buy it with that quarter?"

I must have looked confused,
but my dad said "Take your time and think about it.
Do you have enough money to buy the chocolate bar?"

I said strongly "I have more than enough!
But I don't want to give you my quarter.
That's way too much money!"

My dad smiled and said
"Think about your math—think about subtracting now.
If you give me your quarter,
and I give YOU my dime AND the chocolate bar,
then you'll only have really paid 15 cents—
just the right amount.

This is subtraction in action.
This is called "making change.""

He continued "Money is not the most important thing in this world,
but it is important.
Everything costs money.
And knowing how to handle your money, and get it right,
is very, very important.

If you understand your math, you'll handle your money well.
It's as simple as that.
If you get your math right—if you get your money right—
you'll be in a good place."

His emphasis was certainly not on the value of money,
nor on the spending power of money,
nor on the materialism of money,
rather, it was on the importance
of accurate handling of money.

My dad was simply planting fruit-bearing seeds—
teaching me valuable life-skills in accuracy,
accountability and in stewardship.

At that age, I didn't handle money much at all, for sure,
but somehow,
I really did understand what my dad was saying. I got it.

And I was so happy that he was taking this special one-to-one time with me,
to teach me something important.

I truly sensed the importance of the message,
because my dad was taking time to teach me.
I felt really special
because I easily understood his challenging lesson
about making change.
I knew my dad was pleased with me.
And that counted a lot.

But I quickly changed the subject
because there was something I really didn't understand,
and I desperately wanted to know the answer.
I blurted out "So where is the chocolate bar
that just cost me 15 cents??!!"

He laughed out loudly at my simple child-like focus.
In one way, he knew I was right.
He raised his eyebrows and raised his voice to answer back
"And, just whose money were you spending, Jani??!!"
I laughed too. But I still wanted some chocolate!!!

He continued beaming ear to ear, and he proceeded
to pull out a large chocolate bar from his other pocket.
He handed it to me, saying "Here, have a bite for free.
But the next bite will cost you your own money!!!"

My dad intentionally took some of his precious time
to share his knowledge—share his wisdom—
share his humor and perspective with me—
to encourage me to apply
what I had already been learning in school.

He made learning fun. He made math fun. He made math real.
And, he knew I liked chocolate!
He was able to teach me in a really subtle way,
to value chocolate—that it cost money—
so therefore, I should treasure
each and every tiny little morsel!!!

Thanks be for my dear father,
who cared enough to teach me, to lead me, to equip me,
for life in this beautiful world.
Thanks be for my creative dad,
who just wanted his little daughter
to have every opportunity in life,
to get it right. Amen.

"JUST TELL THE TRUTH"

I never ever wanted to get into trouble with my dad.
It was just so much easier to keep the peace,
and to do what he told me, the way he told me,
when, where and how he told me.
Never asking "Why?" or "How come?."

But, like any other kid my age, I was fairly strong-willed,
and I had a bit of a mind of my own.
If I could do something MY WAY, WITHOUT getting caught,
or, take a shortcut in dad's long list of how-to's,
or, pray tell, not do it at all, you bet I tried!
And I could just tell a little white lie
and say "Yup, I did it Dad,
just like you showed me."

And I'd get caught. Of course I'd get caught!!
My errors were pointed out sternly by old eagle eyes Dad.
He'd say "Jan, you're lying. I can tell you're lying.
Just tell me the truth!"

In punishment, I was then made to repeat my tasks or chores "the right way."
I was sent to my room, or, my allowance was withheld,
or, my privileges were withdrawn
every time I messed up or failed, in my father's eyes.

My dad was no different than any other neighborhood dad.
And, reflective of his RCAF military training—
a place for everything and everything in its place—
he had very high expectations for his little girl.

He taught me standards—his standards.
He set the bar fairly high
because he knew I would probably
achieve or surpass the bar.

He disciplined me strictly,
knowing that the world out there
needed honest and disciplined
leaders and thinkers and workers.

He expected only good work, timely work, and spirited work from me.
No grumbling or complaining. No mouthing off or laziness.
Absolutely no "attitude" was ever tolerated.
And, absolutely only the truth,
and nothing but the truth!!!

Concurrently in my childhood,
there was a TV show called "To Tell the Truth."
I was literally terrified to watch it
because I thought it was all about
catching liars and punishing them!

Enough said.
I learned some of my lessons—a lot of my lessons—the hard way.

But, in looking back, I still thank my dad,
for instilling truth and honesty and a good work ethic in me.
These qualities are all part of the bigger word "integrity"
to which I will always aspire.
My dad taught me well.

May I ever uphold the virtues of truth and honesty,
through all my days.
May we all come to realize their place and importance
in everyday life and living. Amen.

"SO, WHAT DID YOU LEARN?"

In my high-school years, I was a gym rat.
I loved my gym classes and I felt completely at home
trying out for whatever after-school sports
that I was interested in.

In the fall, I played forward—left winger—on the field hockey team.
In the winter months, I was on the gymnastics team,
and I refereed our school volleyball games.
In the spring, I was on the badminton team
and I dabbled with intramural level handball.

More than anything, I enjoyed sports
because I got to train with kids of all grades—
kids who were like-minded in sports,
who weren't in my everyday classrooms.
We weren't the cool kids.
But, we sure had a lot in common.

And, we made our own fun, while working hard, together.
It was great to be part of such a great group of people—aspiring athletes—
goal oriented folks
who enjoyed the highs and lows—
the wins and the losses—
of intercollegiate competition.

In grade 12, I tried out once again, for the badminton team.
Our coach gave us a number of drills
in serving, receiving, network, and rally strategies.

I must say, I took it all in stride,
and with great confidence,
I went through the motions of each drill,
knowing for sure that I'd make the team, again.

The next day after school,
I checked the bulletin board to see who made the team.
When I didn't see my name on the list,
I talked to the coach. I simply said
"I think you forgot to write my name on the list."

In a calm, non-confrontational voice,
she quietly answered my statement,
with a string of soul-searching questions.

"And why do you think that?
Do you think you deserve to be on the team?
Did you honestly put your heart and soul
into the tryouts yesterday?

Did you actually concentrate, and take care to place every single shot?
Were you focused on trying out,
or just randomly hitting at every bird?
Do you think you're better than some of the others—
better than those who DID try their very, very best?

Did you just assume that you'd make the team,
resting on your laurels?
Did you show you cared about your technique,
about bettering your skills and strategies,
about growing as a team player?"

She continued in her kindly voice "Don't answer me now, Janis.
Go home and think about all of this
and come back tomorrow and we'll chat.
But, the posted list is the final list."

I walked home from school alone. I held back my tears.
I think I was in shock.
My first reactions were something like
"How could she do this to me?" and
"She's wrong. I did try hard." and
"How will I ever tell my friends
that I didn't make the team?"

I went straight to my bedroom and closed the door.
No one else was home yet.
My tears flowed.
My sobs were muffled by my pillow.
I felt lost. Wronged.
Hard-done-by. Demeaned.
Stripped of honor. I felt shame.

I had about twenty minutes to myself,
when my dad knocked on my door.
When I didn't answer, right away, he opened the door.

He could see that I had been crying,
and when he sat down beside me, I cried more.
He held me close in a fatherly side-hug,
until my tears subsided.
He said "Are you ready to tell me about it?"

I took a big breath, and recounted the whole story to my dad.
When I repeated the questions that Coach had asked me,
I heard her voice inside my head
calmly, quietly, assertively,
leading my thoughts with her questions.

I stood up after voicing those questions, and I looked at my dad.
Our eyes met in a precious bonding moment.
Silence spoke loudly.
I was coming to a moment of truth.

My tearful soul-searching had brought me to a new level
of self awareness and self understanding—and honesty.
And my dad's listening skills
allowed truth to unfold in the space between us.
I could now see the Light!

I walked across the room to my desk.
I turned around and walked back to my dad.
I paced a few more times,
as I was still working through things in my head.

Coach was right! Dead right! Spot on!
I didn't try hard. I didn't give it my best.
I was casual, and maybe a little overconfident,
and, maybe a little bit cocky.

I wasn't "hoping" to make the team, I was "expecting" to make it.
Not making it, was a huge life-lesson for me.
Not making it, reminded me that no matter what,
I must always try my best—give my very best—do my best.
Not making it, humbled me in a really big way.

My dad was still seated,
looking upward into my eyes, when he gently asked
"So, Jan, what lesson did you learn from all of this?
What is your takeaway?
What will you do differently now?"

I looked away briefly, searching for the right words.
I walked over to the window and looked up to the sky.
Blue sky. Cloudless sky.
Sky full of Light and vastness of space.
Vastness of intrigue.
Wide open vastness.

I turned and looked back at my dad.
He was patiently waiting to help me.
I don't think he expected what I had to say.

I said "Dad, I think I just grew up.
I think I just put a lot of things in perspective.
I am humbled, for sure.

I am just this small person in this great wide world.
When I don't work hard, try hard,
or put a little effort into what I do, my efforts are wasted.

If I want something,
I have to make a goal and match my actions to that goal.
I can't assume. I can't rely on the past. I can't expect.
Here and now, I have to do my best.
I always need to do my best.

I know this is a big world—it's a tough world out there.
And, I won't always get what I want.
And I do need to try—not just sometimes—but always—
I need to try hard to get things done—to have what I need!"

My dad smiled. His gaze was loving and understanding.
He mused . . . to himself . . .
My daughter has just wrestled with some very big questions,
and she has come out on the other side
with grace and maturity and integrity.
In the angst of her high-school trial,
all by herself, she saw the Light.

My dad stood up and held out both hands to me.
I held both of his hands and looked up at him.
Love surrounded us.
Ours was a tender moment.
Mine was a healing moment.
His was affirmation.

His teenager was growing up,
with her head squarely on her shoulders.
He didn't need to counsel or comfort or console.
He just listened,
and Buddy's daughter saw the Light.

May we always try our best.
May we always set attainable goals
and set our sights on achieving them.

May we always reflect on our shortcomings—our failures—our ways—
and stride out, new and improved
and ready to take on the challenges of life.

May we have non-judgmental listeners
and caring compassionate hearts to turn to when we need them.

May we see the Light, ever and always. Amen.

"YOU WANT IT? WORK FOR IT!"

When I was fifteen, strong and sturdy,
my dad asked me, if I would like to have a pool in the backyard.
I was a synchronized swimmer,
and I jumped for joy at the idea!
My dad then said, "Great!
Then you'll work with me to build it!"

We only hired two professional, contracted teams—
the excavators and the cement guys.
We did all the rest of the heavy slugging.

My dad and I assembled and built
all of the vertical steel wall sides and supports.
We laid all of the inflow/outflow pipes
and engineered/MacGyvered
the pool heater into our basement, indoors.

We backfilled behind the steel walls
with umpteen gazillion wheelbarrow loads of gravel.
We did a great job,
and that beautiful pool is still operational today,
some fifty years later,
for the folks now living in our old house.

We wanted a pool.
We were determined to make it happen.
We worked hard to make it happen.

And, our hard work gave us the pleasure—the enjoyment—
of a beautiful backyard paradise—for many years, as a family.

In 1975, in the Fall of my grade thirteen year, I applied to university.
My dad sat me down,
and told me that ever since I was born in 1957,
my parents had been contributing
to a small education fund.

He said it was worth about one thousand dollars,
and that it would likely cover my first year tuition,
books, and transportation costs.

He also said
that if I was going to continue on for more years in university,
that that cost would be my responsibility.
My parents' money would most certainly
get me started,
but I would have to earn the money
to finish a degree.

I did manage to land some well-paying summer jobs as a lifeguard,
between semesters,
and I graduated with my degree in four years.
I worked hard, earned the money I needed,
and got the education I wanted.

Much later on, when I was newly engaged to my husband,
my dad spoke to me again, about money.

It was 1992,
and my parents were willing to put three thousand dollars
toward the cost of the wedding.

If our wedding plans were going to cost more than this,
it would have to be my, and my husband's, responsibility.

We did have a lovely Sunday afternoon wedding ceremony,
and an afternoon tea reception at the church,
followed by a small eighteen-guest
private dining room dinner reception
for the bridal party and the parents.

I set out to sew all of the silken-and-heavily-bejeweled
bridal-and-bridesmaid-dresses.
Our floral choices were simple and tasteful.
We did splurge on a really good photographer.

We were able to have a lovely, Autumn wedding and honeymoon
on a shoestring budget, and we did not go into debt to do so.

My dad's words rang true again,
"If you really, really, really want something badly enough,
you'll be sensible, and you'll work hard to make it happen."

And, a few years later, after we had already poured a lot of money
into a private clinic infertility program,
my husband and I were struggling with the high costs
of the treatments and procedures.

Thankfully my work benefits covered all of the drug costs.
One hundred percent.

My dad dearly wanted us to have kids—HE wanted to be a granddad!!!
He came forward to us,
with an offer of a loan, that would really help us,
and his repayment terms were flexible,
interest-free and very doable.

We never did have any children,
but I'll never forget my dad's generous offers to help us along the way.
The loan was paid back in short order.

How I wish he could have had a grandson or a granddaughter!
He would have been an amazing grandparent!

Pulling all of these little vignettes together,
helps me to see my dad in a really good light.

He planned for the future. Always. And I do too.
He liked to dream big,
and he took the right steps
to help make his dreams come true.

As a fun aside, he was a proud father,
and he was very quick to tell his friends and colleagues,
that I, Buddy's Daughter,
was the very first in his whole family
to graduate with a university degree.
HIS dream came true!

He proudly came from a long line of farmers.
And, having a daughter as a university graduate,
well, this simply made him beam!

My dad knew that hard work always paid off,
and through him, I believe this too.

May I always carry my dad's goal-driven work ethic,
through all my days.
May I continue to hear his voice in my head,
and in my heart,
as I too, work hard,
play hard,
and dream big. Amen.

"MY WAY OR THE HIGHWAY!"

I was a child all of six or seven years of age.
It was the Victoria Day weekend in May, in Canada,
and the neighbors were gathered on the dead-end street
for a multi-family group-effort fireworks display.
The dads were organizing the event.

Families big and small sat huddled on blankets,
and on folding chairs on the lawns.
Ski jackets were worn.
Littler ones were bundled in warm woolen blankets.

Hand held sparklers lay lined up in readiness
on a portable folding table on the driveway.
Dusk was looming. Anticipation was rising.
Cranky kids up way past their bedtimes
were wailing, sobbing and acting out.

I was truly mesmerized by all the hub and bub.
Dad had told me where to sit, and not to move.
Not to run around.
To stay clear of the makeshift fireworks pit on the road.

And so I did. And soon, the show began.
Pop! Whiz! Boom! Bang! Kapow! Poof!
Then, the Burning Schoolhouse!
"Ahhhhh!" "Ohhhhh!" "Ooooooh!"
"Wheeeee!" "Wow!"

Something was moving over there at the fireworks pit,
and it caught my attention.
Without thinking, I got up to go see what it was.
Before I even took three steps,
my dad leaped from behind me
and pulled me—tackled me—down to the ground.
He landed on top of me, protecting me.

In an angry voice, he said
"Jani, you must do things my way—you must listen—
you're going to get hurt if you don't!"
I wasn't shaken, or afraid, but I knew he meant business.
I needed to listen to my dad.

And later that night when another child, Blair, had to go to the hospital
for a facial injury resulting from an exploding firecracker,
I knew that Dad was right.
That could have been me. I knew I had to listen.
I had to learn to do things Dad's way.

Later, when I was seventeen
and Dad was giving me some extra driving practice time
on a nearby suburban street,
I angered my dad once again.

I was approaching a left turn while on a steep downhill road.
No oncoming traffic. No pedestrians. My signal was on,
but I misjudged and entered the corner way too fast,
causing my tires to squeal.

My dad hollered "Brake! Jan, Brake!"
I stopped quickly, and I witnessed his anger rise again.
"You'll never take a corner at that speed again!
You've got to pay attention. Speed kills.
You weren't in control of the car.
You could have hurt or killed someone.
Please. Listen. Do things my way.
You'll be safe!"

I took this moment to heart, and I became a very safety-first, cautious driver.
My dad was right. So very right.
In that moment, I was not in control.
I was not paying attention to my speed.
Lesson learned.

When I was age 20, in university,
I came bouncing home from campus one night,
full of the news of an upcoming class excursion for course credits.

Our class was going skydiving!
The weekend event was one week away.
My dad allowed me at the dinner table to babble on and on
about the trip details, the course instruction costs,
the carpool and travel arrangements,
and the credentials of the teachers.

When I was done, I turned to my dad and said
"So, what do you think Dad?
Can I take the car and go to Newmarket for the weekend,
and get my certifications? Can you help me with the cost?"

My dad was very calm. Very self-assured. Very calculated.
He said "Jan, it sounds like a great course and a great opportunity.
You've covered every detail!
But, I'm sorry. If you choose to jump out of a plane,
you can choose to live somewhere else.

My home isn't open to irresponsible people.
Daredevils. Risk-takers. Or folks who don't value their own life.
You jump. You leave.
My way or the highway."

Of course I didn't take the course.
I was only earning part time wages as a full time student,
and I had no means to pay rent to live on my own
outside of the family home.

Another hard lesson, but, Dad was right.
He wasn't going to approve of anything
that could potentially harm his little girl.
Never, ever, ever.

May I always know and feel the love of my father.
May I understand that his rules,
"My way or the highway," were made
based on love, and wisdom, and safety-first.

I pray that all children could know the love of a father,
whose love was unconditional,
whose love kept them safe from all harm. Amen.

FAMILY TIME

Family, was everything to my dad.
He felt a powerful connection
and had a real sense of contentment
when we were all together. Key words—all together!

Whether we were simply sharing a meal together,
or doing chores as a team
around the house on Saturday mornings,
or traveling in the car across the Skyway Bridge
to do some Christmas shopping in Hamilton,
he found great joy
in our being together—all together.

This in time became increasingly difficult
as us kids took on part time jobs in our later teenage years,
or, especially with me training at the pool
or attending out of town field hockey tournaments.
In my dad's eyes, we all lost out
when one of us was absent,
for any length of time.

My dad had a brilliant idea.
If he were to purchase a small property up north,
on the edge of a golf course
that had a clubhouse, pool and bar,
we could all go up there on weekends—
together.

There was lots to do!
Fishing on the Black River and in Lake Simcoe,
swimming in the pool, golf,
reading books on the hammock by the riverside.
Endless cross country skiing in the winters!!!

Meals would be prepared by the clubhouse chef,
so Mom wouldn't have to plan meals, cook meals,
and clean up after meals all weekend long.
She could relax with the rest of us.
It was a Win-Win plan!

Except, it wasn't.
Dad went up north religiously on weekends
to care for the gardens, chat with the neighbours,
golf, fish, and relax.
But mostly, he was there alone.

Us kids were now in university with lots of reading and studying,
exams, and papers due. Endless papers due.
Mom was never much of an outdoors enthusiast
so she didn't go north
unless we were all going to be there.
Sadly, my dad spent hours, many weekends,
at his beautiful home away from home,
alone.

We were all sad in witnessing this. His brilliant plan was backfiring.
What he wanted most in life was slowly slipping away,
simply due to the natural evolution
of family-lived-experience over time.

We were dispersing, dissipating, disconnecting as a family unit,
and we were powerless to change it.

May we all know in our hearts that truly connected feeling—
that togetherness feeling—
that feeling of belonging
and being part of something special, like a family.

May we all honor and cherish family time,
and the family ties which bind our hearts through all time.

May we all strive like my dad, Buddy,
to live out our family lives,
strengthened and comforted by the joy of family time.

For those who do not have such a family bond,
may they still seek out and find the joy and the comforts
of true connectedness and belonging,
with their "chosen people,"
in their own "chosen family circle,"
throughout their daily living. Amen.

COLD HARD TRUTHS—
Racism, Prejudice and Discrimination

Caution: Reactive language and sensitive material contained.
Reader discretion is advised.

Sad to say, my dad spoke his mind. Always.
  If he didn't like something, or someone, he said so.
    If he didn't like what you just did, he told you.
      If he didn't understand something,
        he showed contempt.

If something or someone was different,
  he was openly vocal and reactive, about their difference.

And especially in his teenage years,
  if his pals were acting out in herd behaviors,
    he was often part of the herd. Strength in numbers.

And I think his contempt only got worse in the Air Force.
  He had bad things to say
    about the visible-and-not-so-visible-minorities.

Name calling, racial slurs, cultural and language intolerance
  were all parts of the military culture of the time—
    unacceptable, but true.
      And this became a style—a signature style—
        of his own contemptuous personhood.

No one ever corrected him on his remarks or on his stance.
  No one ever dared to stand up to his obvious ignorance.

He was proud to say that he was just as opinionated as his own dad, Chester.
In my dad's world,
the Maritime First Nations Mi'kmaq, were "those damn Injans."
Black folks were "Spooks."
Italians were the "I-Ties,"
and the Chinese and Japanese
were "Chinks and Japs."

I'm sure that part of his approach was shades of sarcasm,
and sick humor,
but truly, therein,
was a deep-seated dislike
for anyone who was different.

He even mocked the Orthodox Jewish people,
calling them "the Hairy Jews."
The French Canadians were "Frogs."

In the seventies, when there was an influx
of new immigrants into our local neighborhoods,
the new targets of his slander and contempt
were "the Pollack's, the Paki's and the Geeks."
He loved Archie Bunker's racist rants.

It is very very hard for me to pen this reflection.
It speaks of a time—an era—a generational attitude—
of blatant white supremacist thinking and idealism.

It speaks largely to the widespread insensitivities
of the white-washed world of mid-century North America.

As a young school-aged child, I called out my dad many times,
saying "Dad, you can't say things like that anymore."
And later as a teenager, I said, "Dad, you've got it all wrong.
The folks you are talking about
are human beings,
just like you and me,
and they have feelings too.

How dare you speak like that, or think like that. The world is changing.
And you have to change with it. Stop being so prejudiced!"

And, the icing was put on the cake in the Spring of grade 11.
I decided to go on a summer French exchange program
to Rimouski, Quebec.
I would stay with a French-speaking family in July,
and my French exchange partner, Michelle,
would then come to live with us
in Toronto, for a month in August.

When I told my dad about the opportunity, he scoffed at me loudly
"Why on earth would you want to learn French by immersion?
What are you thinking?
Why would you want to learn that crap anyway?!

The government is bad enough for ramming
French bilingual signage
and bilingual packaging down our throats,
and now, you want to bring French into our home?

I don't care what you do, but don't expect me to speak Frog!"

I guess it wasn't easy for my dad,
watching the world's new "intolerance of intolerance,"
change before his eyes,
watching all of his familiar social mores undergo radical conversions,
watching the red carpets of tolerance, sensitivity, and unity
being rolled out before all of the minority groups, in the 70's.

Eventually later in life, he became much less overt—much less vocal—
and he often held his tongue.
His discrimination simply went underground.
He came to know his new place in life,
as a closet bigot.
I don't think he changed his thinking very much,
he was just way-way-way-less-in-anyone's-face
with his intolerance and contempt.

My dad was no saint, that's for sure.
Our views and approaches may have been very divergent,
but he's still my dad, I'm still his little girl.
I'm Buddy's Daughter alright—and I speak my truth.
I'm Buddy's strong voice, with Jani's heart!

I still love my dad, despite his flaws and faults and all.
I can separate the man and his actions.
I can and I do separate the man from his words—
his heart from his head.
I can and I do forgive him,
and all of his contempt,
and his derogatory racist speech.

Change can only come about,
when we learn from our mistakes of the past—
when we move forward with integrity and conviction,
to do better—to be better—to better the world.

Right or wrong, good or bad, my dad was a man of his time.
My dad was a man who always spoke his mind,
in the face of a world that was changing right before him.
The world became more sensitive—became color blind—
while he remained openly opinionated and frank.
And sadly, hurtful too.

May we all stand up tall—taller—
and then say and do the right things,
in the face of racism, prejudice,
discrimination, and social injustice.
And then, may we see the dawning
of loving, and respectful
neighbors and neighborhoods,
all around the world.
May we live to see this in our lifetime.
Amen.

“WHY ARE YOU ASKING ME?’

Caution: Reactive language and sensitive material contained.
Reader discretion is advised.

In the 1970’s, a shy young man named Jeff worked with my dad.
He had a big question on his heart, and one day,
he asked my dad at the picnic table at lunchtime
“Bud, what if I’m gay?”

Totally caught off guard, and mortified,
my dad at age fifty, said in his gruff voice,
“Why are you asking me??!!”

The young man sat waiting for more of a retort, more of a battering.
There was no more.
Quietly, thoughtfully, earnestly,
Jeff proceeded with extreme caution.

He said “My own dad is a tough guy. Farmer tough. Backwoods tough.
He’d probably beat me. He wouldn’t understand.
He’d holler long and loud,
and he wouldn’t hear another word I’d have to say.
He’d dismiss me. Probably disown me.

I’m asking you, Bud, because you’ve always been a good listener.
You treat me like a son.
I trust you, Bud.”

Dad immediately softened.
But his heart was still racing—he was panicking.
This young lad was coming to my dad
for advice on a sensitive matter—
one about which my dad
was not at all comfortable talking.

Recent radio and newspaper headlines
had blurted and blared and boasted
about gay bashings,
about the growing downtown gay community,
and the new gay bars.

The words "coming out" were understood by only-a-few-in-the-know.

My dad knew only what the newspapers said.
He didn't have a clue about same-sex relationships or gender identity—
there was no common vocabulary yet in the 1970's,
for this subject.
Dad felt like a fish out of water.
He was conflicted.
He couldn't breathe.

But then, he looked in the young man's eyes.
He saw honesty. He saw trust. He saw hope.
Jeff had come to my dad, looking for answers—
looking for support—looking for fatherly advice.
Jeff had felt safe with his co-worker friend in Bud.

My dad got a hold of his fears—
of his own wild and racing thoughts—
and he managed to collect himself, and to cool his jets.

Dad said "I don't know how to answer that, Jeff. All I can do is listen.
That's all I know how to do.
What you're going through—
whatever you're going through—
I cannot begin to understand.

I'll take back my words 'Why are you asking me?'
That was harsh, and I'm sorry.
But, I can see that you're carrying a big load on your shoulders.

I like you Jeff, as a person, as a friend.
So, I can help—I will help—by listening.
I cannot make decisions for you, or offer intelligent answers.
These are your questions to work through, and, I will listen.
I hope this is okay for you?

Jeff sat quietly. His tears welled up.
He was overcome
by the expressive humanity of my dad's stance.

Jeff sensed my dad's discomfort—and his reactive contempt.
But, Jeff also saw a human being.
He saw a human being, being a human being.

He saw a person reaching out despite the awkwardness—
despite the dis-ease—
to show care and concern—and respect—to another.
A person who could veritably look into his eyes
and see a burdened soul weighed down
by social malevolence, disdain, and injustice.

A person who could rise above his own controversies
to take time to comfort a friend in need.

Jeff and my dad remained friends
for many more years at their workplace.
Their lunchtime conversations were all over the board—
both superficial and deep—
as the situations dictated.
Dad listened, intently.
Theirs was truly
a father-son relationship,
without any bonds
of shared DNA.

My dad worked until he was 72. He loved his work.
Not long after my dad retired, he died in 2000.

Jeff approached me at the funeral reception.
He wanted me to know that my dad
had helped him through some very dark times.

He said that my dad had saved him.
My dad's willingness to simply be
a non-confrontational and non-judgmental listening ear,
was the greatest gift that Jeff had ever received.

Might we all learn to listen—
and know to listen—
truly listen—
at the right time.

Might we all reach beyond our comfort zones,
at the right time,
in the name of compassion, respect and tolerance—
in the name of humanity.

Might we all
become more/most fully human.
May we all vow,
to human better. Amen.

P.S., Dad always gave me eye contact,
looked deeply into my soul,
and listened to my heart,
throughout our lives together.
He was a man of few words.
He was deeply sensitive
to the needs of his kids.

No wonder Jeff felt so comfortable with my dad.
Dad's really, really, really, big heart was human—all human. Amen.

A SCARY MOMENT

Caution: Reactive language and sensitive material contained.
Reader discretion is advised.

We can never, ever, fully understand what someone else is going through,
unless we are their confidante, their go-to, their life-line.

My dad often kept details to himself. Need to know only.
He protected us kids from so much worry
and from fears of the unknown.

We only knew that he got a new job,
never that his previous employer
was downsizing and laying off half of the staff.

We never knew just how much he budgeted, scrimped and saved—
and how he simply 'did without'—
just to make ends meet on a month to month basis.

Family finances were his business, his burden.
Not ours.
And I'm thankful that I grew up worry-free,
carefree, unburdened. Stress-free.
I had an idyllic childhood.

But, this came at a price.
In my dad not communicating his feelings,
or sharing his thoughts and fears,
his emotions would often be bottled up,
and once in a while, they'd explode.

The worst I ever witnessed, is hard for me to even write down.

Our family dog, Gidget,
was a silver-grey toy poodle, all of twelve pounds.
She was a quiet dog most of the time, but once in a while,
something outdoors—a bunny, squirrel or chipmunk—
would get her going,
and she'd be at the living room window,
barking incessantly at the culprit.

Well, one day my dad had barely gotten home from work,
suit and tie worn, briefcase in hand, and Gidget started up.
She had already greeted him warmly
on his arrival in the foyer of our home,
with licks and wags
and her gleeful puppy excitement.

But, then she ran up the six steps to the living room
to bark incessantly at something outdoors. She was yapping loudly.
The volcano was about to blow.
Whatever was going on in my dad's world—
in his heart—in his mind—at his workplace—
just made him snap. He lost it.

He dropped his briefcase on the floor, with a bang.
He marched up the six stairs
and grabbed Gidget by the scruff of her neck.
She squealed in pain.

He walked to the head of the stairs
and drop-kicked her like a football,
across the hall into the main-floor laundry room.
She landed with a thud and became silent.

When he went down the stairs to close—
to slam—the laundry room door, he turned to me saying
"And don't you go in there. She needs to learn a lesson."

I was frightened. I obeyed.
I didn't want to upset my dad any more than he already was.
I had never seen him this angry.
I had never seen him "lose it."
When he went up to the kitchen,
I went outside and I cried.
I didn't understand.

And since then in my life,
at times I have personally experienced that "bottled up" feeling.
And thankfully I recognized it
before I did anything like drop-kick an innocent dog.

I learned a really big life-lesson that day, in a sickening, ugly way.

I wish my dad had learned that very same lesson
way, way, way earlier on in his life.
To this day, I cannot unsee his rage.
I cannot unsee the misdirected anger.
I cannot unsee him drop-kicking our sweet Gidget.

If you have bottled up feelings,
find someone you trust, and share your feelings
openly, honestly, and in a timely manner.
Open yourself. Trust that folks will listen and care.
You do not have to go the journey alone. You are not alone.
Share your burdens. Confide. Spill your beans.
Promise me this.

May we always learn the lessons we need to learn, in a timely way.
May we always learn from our lessons—and learn them well—
be they big or small, tough or easy,
or just plain painful to swallow.

And, let us not dwell in the dark days of our past.
May we always grow through our darkness, into the Light. Amen.

P.S., Our wee Gidget was not injured at all. No broken ribs or limbs. And, thankfully, she continued to love my dad unconditionally. She adored him, no matter what. God bless our wee Gidget.

BUDDY'S LAMENT

My dad, "Buddy" was "all guy."
Strong and sturdy from his early years on the farm.
He loved all things mechanical, electrical, engineerable—
"MacGyverable."

Saturday afternoon football games and Hockey Night in Canada on TV.
Summertime fishing and golfing.
Spring and Fall air shows, and fly-ins,
automotive shows and boating shows.

He was the proud daddy of two lovely young girls, my sister and me.
We were most definitely "all-girl girls"—
one synchro swim athlete, and one bookworm.
Tried as he did, we didn't share in his enthusiasm,
for his "all-guy pursuits."

He bought a gated property, one hour north of Toronto,
when us girls were in university, hoping to create some special family times
in his little home away from home.
There was, right on the property, a nine-hole golf course,
a river ripe for sport fishing.
And, an outdoor pool just like at home.

Even a members-only dining room, outdoor BBQ, and bar!

But, with our studies and our part time jobs,
the plan back-fired,
and he spent many many weekends up north, all alone.

He loved us girls, but deep in his heart, he lamented.
He had truly longed for a son—
a son to share in his "all-guy" passions,
to go fishing with, to talk shop with.
A son who was naturally mechanically inclined—
a son after his own heart.

Time and years moved forward, and there would be no son.
The writing was on the wall.
He lived in a clearly estrogen-driven household—
an estrogen-stronghold.

Dad never ever openly expressed his desires,
but we the family all knew what a difference it would have made,
if we all could just "talk-guy" with our dad!

Then the miracle happened!
Out of the blue in 1987, I brought a boyfriend home,
who in five years time would become Dad's only son-in-law.

Dad and Barry hit it off immediately,
and they were often found together after work, beers in hand,
deep in conversation
about motors, or horsepower,
or power trim, or digital depth finders.

They became fast friends. They had a common vocabulary.
They shared inside jokes, and dry humor.

What a blessing for Dad,
that he truly had the son (-in-law) relationship
that he had dreamed of. Finally!
They had thirteen years
of connecting over guy things—
thirteen years of a very special
"all-guy world."

My dad passed away after a one-week admission
  to the palliative care ward.
    He was made comfortable.
      IV morphine was his new best friend.
        He was coherent, until the very last 16 hours.

At four o'clock of the day before my dad would pass,
  I was sitting quietly at the bedside,
    while my dad slept, snoring loudly.

Barry entered the room. Dad awakened, and greeted Barry,
  with a jolly, happy, genuine grin, ear to ear,
    and a really big wave.
      They Hi-fived!

What a beautiful moment!
  They both nodded. No words were spoken.
    They shared something deep—they shared in silence.

My dad slipped into a coma,
  just after this tender moment.
    It was one of the sweetest moments ever.

Dad remained in a coma overnight
  and he took his last breath
    at eight AM the next morning.
      Comfortable. Peaceful.
        At peace.

My dad secretly longed, languished—lamented.
  He had prayed for a lifetime, for a son.
    And late in life, he was blessed with "the gift of a son."
      His soul was smiling.
        And his heart was full of gratitude.

Might we all hope for, wish for, and pray for,
that which will complete us, and make us whole.
And, might our petitions, pleas and prayers,
be answered, at the last.
May we all come into wholeness,
through our faith in God,
in God's time. Amen.

FRVSNT

In the 1980's, when I first met my husband-to-be, Barry,
he'd often comment on my natural inner sparkle,
my exuberance, my *joie de vivre,*
and my contagious energy.
He then gave me the affectionate nickname,
"Effervescent"!

And, sometimes in jest,
he'd mention me in a funny story among friends,
referring to me as his "Eff-ing wife"! LOL! Ahaha!

He has a great sense of humor, a really big heart,
and, he knows me well.
Who could ever ask for anything more?

In traveling to Nova Scotia,
to meet my large extended family a few years after our wedding,
Barry sat down over a pot of tea—or ten!—
with my aunts, uncles, cousins,
and some of their really great neighbors.

They were all gracious, open-hearted,
fun-loving, and talkative,
in a sharing, friendly, down-home kind of way.
Barry then said out loud
"Now I know! Now I get it!

Janis' "way of being" is not solely a "Janis-thing,"
it's a down-east, down-home, downright-damn-good thing!
These Eastern folks are all bubbly, and happy,
and energized—and energizing.
They're all effervescent!
I see it so clearly now.
Janis comes by it so naturally!"

To this very day,
I am honored to wear my tiny, thin gold wedding band,
lovingly inscribed on the inside with the words
"For my FRVSNT Love."

Thanks be to God for Barry,
who knows me,
who knows my heart,
and who loves me all the same.
Ours is indeed,
an FRVSNT Love. Amen.

FORMING ME SOFTLY WITH HIS WORDS

"I believe in you, Jan. You should too."
In January 2000, my dad spoke softly
as we stood in the foyer of Mom and Dad's tiny condo.

My dad's prognosis was grim. Surgery was not an option.
Chemo might work if he could tolerate the side effects.
Maybe only a couple of months until . . .

I look back at that time in my life
and at the prospect of losing my dad to cancer,
wondering what life would be like without my dad.
It didn't look good at all, then, from my perspective.

But my dad's words were not new to me.
For in fact, I grew up my whole life—well into my forties—
knowing that he believed in me.

I grew up with him teaching me and reminding me—and showing me—
that if I put my mind to something and really worked at it,
I would be richly rewarded for my efforts.
He truly equipped me to face life—
boldly, smartly and keenly.

And his words formed me. Shaped me. Created me.
He made me who I am today—
strong, capable, independent and resourceful.

And so much more. For all of this, my heart is full. So very full.

And as I sit here in the midwinter twilight of 2025,
absolutely glowing from within
with yet another exquisite success in hand,
I look up and I listen.

In the quiet, in the stillness, in the twinkling light,
I hear my father's words,
and the love and encouragement in his voice,
"No doubts. No fears.
Go forward with your eyes on the goal,
and make it yours. You can do this Jan.
Just believe that you can,
and you will."

Sigh . . . I love you Dad, and I miss you.
I only wish that I had a son or a daughter to teach,
as you have so lovingly taught me.

Thanks be to God for fathers who believe in their children,
who *love their children into dreams-come-true,*
who *believe their children into being their very best selves.*

Thanks be to God for my father, Buddy.
I am so honored to be his daughter—Buddy's Daughter. Amen.

BUDDY—THE SHADOW YEARS

My older sister, BJ, was frail and unwell most of her life.
She lived with my parents, her whole life.
Her life was limited,
and restricted, in so many ways.

She had a number of medical conditions,
the long-term life-sustaining medications for which
had caused multiple predictable complications.

And, way too soon at age thirty-eight,
she slipped away to the heavens—
into her Holy Rest—
with her loving God.

My dad hated hospitals. I never really knew just why.
So, for most of my sister's admissions to the medical wards
or to the intensive care units,
Mom and I were the visitors,
and we would relay updates and details
to my dad, back at home.
And, my being a nurse on staff
surely helped a lot.

Of course he would speak to doctors on the phone,
and at doctor's office appointments,
but he just couldn't bring himself to go to the hospital,
to visit his BJ.

He never said so, but I'm sure my dad was burdened
with the guilt of failing to be with his daughter
through the long endless hours, in her times of need.
In his eyes, he failed to be with her, in saying goodbye.
He couldn't help it.
He couldn't help her.

My dad was seventy when BJ died,
and so began the lengthening shadows—
life in the shadows—
the great shades and shadows of sadness—
depression with a capital D.

My dad was still working because he loved his job.
But after BJ died, he lost his love for work—
he lost his drive and his will—
he lost his *joie de vivre* and his *raison d'etre.*
Pardon my French, Dad.

He felt restless, agitated, lost.
He needed to squelch his restless mind,
to calm his on-edge nerves,
to still his soul, and numb his physically painful grief.

Two years later, he decided to stop working—
he finally retired—at age seventy-two.
He had completely lost his sense of purpose—
lost his pride in his personhood,
and in his self-worth.

He began to drink. All day.
He took sleeping pills—during the day.
Day after day, hour after hour,
he sat alone in the den,
in his deep-seated armchair,
stoned and empty and blank.

He called me to his side one day,
  and finally shared what was on his heart.
    He missed his daughter—his BJ—so very much.
      She had always needed him,
        and he truly needed to be needed.

He broke into a surging waterfall of tears
  as he poured out those words.
    He felt he just wasn't needed anymore.

I reminded him that both Mom and I were still there,
  and we still needed him—
    in many different ways from BJ's neediness,
      but we still, needed him.

I needed my strong, wise, savvy dad
  to lead me, to guide me, advise me—
    to support and encourage me
      in my own budding plans and hopes and dreams.
        My mom still needed her best friend,
          her confidante, her love.

Dad just shook his head and said
  "You don't understand—you'll never understand.
    Part of me died when BJ died.
      Her special needs are what kept me going,
        what kept me driven,
          what gave me purpose.

Everything I've done, I've done for her.
  I worked all these extra years
    to build a comfortable nest egg for her,
      for when I'm gone—
        to cover her medical needs when I'm gone.

All my life, I've budgeted and scrimped and saved
  and I've gone without many things,
    all in the name of providing for BJ.
      She was my life. And now I have nothing."

My heart went out to my dad, for finally sharing in frankness,
the depths of his heart-wrenching, gut-wrenching pain.
For finally bringing Light into the darkness of his world.
But I felt something more. Way, way, way more.

I was suddenly realizing
that my dad just couldn't see my own needs for him.
Our needs for him.
He was truly blind to reality.

His grief was literally blinding him to the love that surrounded him,
and to the needs that we had for him—
the needs that connected us so very deeply to him.

He only knew the darkness, the shadows,
and the anguish of grief—of loss.
He was totally oblivious
to the wonders of our special relationship.
And this revelation hurt me.

It ached and burned and weighed in my heart.
It was stabbing my heart—
disabling my heartbeat and the flow of my lifeblood—
breaking me—
bringing me down, down, down.

He never really pulled himself out of this slump—
this sadness,
this hole of darkness,
this sucking mud hole—sinkhole—of grief.

At age seventy-five, he got the diagnosis of inoperable lung cancer.
He endured three rounds of chemo,
and he died a very lonely and broken man.

I was at his hospital bedside, 24/7, in his last week of life.
I needed to be there.
For him. For me. For real.

I wish I could have changed the end of his life-story.
I wish I could have made it all better.
I wish I could have taken his grief and turned it around,
and led him out of the darkness, back into the Light.

But I didn't. I couldn't. And not for lack of trying.
Dad's vow to keep his daughter—my sister—
happy, healthy and well, and safe at all cost—
could not be upheld.

He crumbled to pieces with his gnawing sense of failure.
And this pained my heart deeply.
I wish he could know just how much he meant to me.
How I looked up to him.
How I truly needed him.
How I valued him.
How I loved him.

Perhaps herein lies an unstated purpose of this book—
therapy for my own fragile heart—
therapeutic "remedial" writing—
restorative therapy for my soul.

May we all know the deepest depths
of love, connectedness, and interconnectedness.

May we all be driven to serve each other, to love each other,
like fathers and daughters, mothers and sons,
like siblings for each other.
Like family through all life,
just as God loves us, unconditionally,
through all time. Amen.

COMMENTARY

LIFE

Life is fluid, dynamic, unbridled.

Life in the moment is chaotic, kaleidoscopic, and free.
Life over time, is mountaintop-high and broad-valley-low.
Life itself is oceanic, cosmic—deep and vast and wild.
Yet, it is intimate, tender, and sweet.

The river of life meanders, gurgles, and churns—
forward, intrepid, sure.
The Light of life shines—shines brightly.
The essence of life is mystery—beautiful Holy Mystery.

Wise words from the poet of yesteryear now grace my tongue . . .
"Come forth into the Light of things—Let Nature be your teacher."[2]

Know the good life.
Come to know joy, in the vastness of living life out loud.
Live and breathe your best life, in appreciative wonder,
in all of life's precious moments.

Life blesses. Life teaches. Life gives.
Life breathes. Life lives.
Life is good. Life is very, very good. Amen.

2. William Wordsworth, "The Tables Turned" in *Lyrical Ballads*, 20.

NAMASTE

My astute and worldly-wise Celtic Wisdom professor
would always greet and bid farewell to his students,
with the word 'Namaste',
spoken while bowing to them in utmost reverence.

The origin of the word 'Namaste' is indeed Sanskrit, ancient,
yet it fully, wholly and completely embodies the core teaching
of the ancient Celtic Wisdom.
Let East meet West—and North, and South!

'Namaste' is truly a cross-cultural sentiment,
full of depth, and so very befitting for use
in our modern-day spiritual-seeking-soul-searching world.

Simply offering 'Namaste'
brings a welcomed wash of hushed enlightenment
into our very being, in the moment.
Eastern origin, yes!
Broadly utilized, yes, yes!
Universal appeal, yes, yes, yes!

'Namaste . . . the Sacred in me honors the Sacred in you.'
Simple. Powerful. Real. True.

The ancient Celtic Wisdom acknowledges
that all life and living are born of God,
that all life and living are indeed, Sacred.

When I bow to you, and quietly offer 'Namaste' to you,
it's a humbling moment—
a very special connecting
of our souls, of our Sacredness, of our inner Lights.

Oh, that every connection we make, verbal or non-verbal,
could reach out—reach in—reach toward—
the shared Sacredness in our midst!

We might all breathe easier, feel safer, feel more valued,
if we all knew that every connection, verbal or non-verbal,
that we made in our everyday daily living,
was born of reverence,
arose out of respect,
and was guided gently
on the wings of love
and compassion!

We all might come to know
what living in harmony, in unity, in peace, really looks like,
if we were always, always, always,
seeking the Sacred in "the other",
in so doing, treating "the other"
with respect, compassion and love.

We might all move towards
communal joy, contentment, Oneness.
I pray for these times.

Let me always bow, to the other.
Let me truly see the other,
truly see them,
in the Light of their inborn Sacredness—
in the wonder of their inborn Sacredness.

Let me approach all life and living—freely and in reverence—
with respect, in compassion, and in love.
May the world reclothe itself in reverence,
one Namaste at a time. Amen.

Namaste . . . Amen.

LET US ALL, MOTHER WELL

Don't we all have a mothering spirit?
It's really hard for me to think otherwise!
But then, that's me!

Mothering as a word, is as broad as it is deep.
It is as specific as it is nebulous.
It is as real as it is imagined.

Mothering is a feel good word.
We all, have had a mom. We've all been mothered.

She was the first one we ever turned to,
in joy, in fear, in hunger, in insecurity.
We settled in her very presence,
and at the sound of her voice,
and at the scent of her loving embrace.

Mothering is truly an action word, and, it also has a passive nuance.
Let your heart wander and meander
with this simple notion!

Mothering for most is natural, instinctive and inborn.
Place an infant precariously (God forbid!) somewhere in the room,
and watch all of the mothering energies in the room
cascade upon the wee one—
protective, concerned, righteous,
altruistic, benevolent, humane,
compassionate, tender, loving.

Mothering itself is just as diverse in style,
as cultures are diverse across the whole wide world.
And this is okay!

There is no perfect way of mothering.
There is no perfect mother.
There is no perfect curriculum for mothering.

There are many givens in mothering.
Provider of love and comfort.
Provider of basics—shelter, food and water.
Encourager. Leader and role model. Teacher.
Fellow dancer and playpal.
Both monster chaser and dream chaser!

And daddies can mother too! Aunties can mother.
Lady-next-door can mother.
Strangers can mother.
Teachers and librarians and dance teachers and music teachers
and Sunday School teachers
and nurses and doctors and bakery-store-ladies can all mother—
they can all mother well.

Scholars speak of masculine energies and feminine energies.
They are both necessary for the universe to flow onward,
to thrive in beautiful balance.
These energies are life-sparks.
They are truly Sacred.
They are real.
The mothering spirit—the Sacred feminine—
is an integral part of the whole of humanity.

Children can sense the mothering spirit of their fathers.
Children know when and by whom they are being mothered,
and in response,
they will draw close to those who mother them well.

Let us come to understand the power of the mothering spirit.
Let us all attune to our mothering spirit,
arising from deep within us.
Let us claim this mothering spirit as part of our identity,
part of our whole,
and let us see mothering
as something that truly defines us all.

May our mothering spirit
graciously nurture, protect, lead and prosper "this generation,"
and all generations to come.
May we all, mother well. Amen.

BEYOND

What is beyond?
A place? A space? A time? A realm? A dimension?
Real or perceived? Or conjured, imagined—fantasized?!
A practice of mind? A presence of mind? A piece of mind?

Beyond doubt. Beyond question. Beyond the hills. Beyond the stars.
Beyond expectations. Beyond our dreams.
Beyond our comprehension. Beyond reality.
Beyond perfection. Beyond all time and Eternity.

Farther. Wider. Higher. Deeper. A reach. A stretch. A grasp.
Reachable and attainable for the artist, poet and dreamer.
Yet, simply out of the question
for the realist, the pragmatist,
and the purist black-and-white.

Totally exasperates, or whimsically charms.
Dulls into despair, or effervesces with hope.

Let us grow in wonder and what-if.
Let us thrive in limitless appreciation.
Let us breathe—in joy and in hope and in lightness of spirit.
Let us live, in beyond. Amen.

RESTLESS—WE THREE

"I was born restless!" she answered.
"Born to question, born to yearn, born to wonder, born to learn.
Born to travel, quest and ride, born to seek wide open skies."

Then she quoted Tennyson, almost word for word—
these words were long-time-etched upon her heart:
"I cannot rest from travel, I will drink life to the lees . . .
I am a part of all that I have met . . .
(I'm) always roving with a hungry heart."[3]

I listened in awe and wonder, and in delight.
I soaked in her message, her spirit, her Light.

And in the gentle noontime breeze amid woodpeckers in the trees,
I sensed—I knew—and now I see—
that she—that Ulysses—and me—we three are free—so free.

The heart of Ulysses lives on!

May we all, may we ever be . . .
Free to question, free to yearn, free to wonder, free to learn.
Free to travel, quest and ride, free to seek wide-open skies. Amen.

3. A. L. Tennyson, "Ulysses" in *Poems by A.L. Tennyson, Volume 2*, unnumbered pages.

ON OUR WAY . . .

We're all on our way.
Stepping up. Stepping out. Striding out.
Our steps are simply points in time and place—
markers to our moments—markers to our now.
We are walking in the Light of now.

Left foot, right foot.
Left then right—one step at a time—one day at a time—
on our pathway to becoming more/most fully human—
on our daily faith journey—
on our grand lifelong odyssey
of spiritual formation.

Wind in our faces—
storm after storm—
we trudge, we lean into, bracing.
Then, wind at our backs and sun on our shoulders—
gentle and warm—we pause, Lovelight gracing.

Rocky and rugged and weathered the roads—
uphill and down.
Rocky and rugged and weathered the shores—
seaspray abounds.

Sometimes the fog drifts in low, obscuring our path—our way is a blur.
Sometimes the path divides—we must decide—to go or return.

"We all have promises to keep
  And miles to go before we sleep"[4]
    And in our hearts these words repeat.

Still, earth turns and time rolls, and eternity billows and flows—
  forward, onward—
    unwavering and undaunted—unfolding.
      Our hearts—beholding.

Yes, we're all on our way.
  We're well on our way.
    Path or no path. Crooked or plain.
      Vision distorted or crystal clear.

Eternity grounds us.
  Eternity beckons us—calling us—here and now. Amen.

4. Robert Frost, "Stopping by Woods on a Snowy Evening" in *New Hampshire*, 87.

MOVING FORWARD

Life itself can be likened to the cycles of preparation and competition
leading up to the Olympics, every four years.

Goal setting is key.
Small interim goals need to be set and achieved
in the in-season-and-off-season-local-and-worldly-events.
Personal goals,
versus tactical goals and strategies,
versus high-performance-in-the-moment-tweaking—
these all matter.

They matter enough to become the centering core
of the whole of the athlete's life—
of our own lives.

Like the winter Olympic skating, team pursuit event,
sometimes we need our teammate drafting right behind us,
their physical presence simply driving us from behind,
to help propel us forward,
to keep us on pace and on track,
and heading us toward the finish line—
our finish line—
our ultimate goal.
Key word—Goal.

They move forward with us, striding out and gliding out.
Breathing with us—they ride with us in the race of our lifetime.
Key word—With-Us.

Or, sometimes we need to be in the short track skating team relay,
where our own teammate, at the precise moment,
gives us the hands-on timely butt-push from behind
that we so need, to shift gears and take over,
to burst forward with new energy,
resolve, commitment and drive—
to cross the finish line,
having given our best,
in the performance of our lifetime.
Key word—Teammate.

Sometimes we respond at our very best,
as the curling skip hollers out so loud and long, repetitively,
HARD !!!,
or in contrast, to the soft-spoken whispered timely cue word,
UP!
by the rinkside figure skating coach in the silent arena
during the freeskate warm-up time.
Key word—Coach.

Sometimes, we simply need a friend, someone who knows our heart,
and cares for us with understanding and compassion.
In their deep listening, they support us—
they can truly hear our heart.
Key word—Friend.

Without goals or direction, without coaching and assistance,
without the support of friends and those who love us,
we go nowhere, fast.
Life can seem to drift,
fall apart, fail to progress, fall backward.

We all need to look at our lives—
learning from the mistakes of yesteryear,
knowing ourselves fully in the moment of the present,
and setting our sights
on the potentials and possibilities of tomorrow.

We need to wake up to the power
of being in the driver's seat of our own lives.
And we need to rise up in this power to set our course,
find our way, make our way,
and arrive,
as the person in the place and space and time
that we always believed we could be.

This mindset is for everyone.
Absolutely everyone.

Single moms of impressionable tender children.
Assembly line workers. Sanitation Engineers.
High powered business executives.
Leaders. Followers. Teachers. Volunteers.
Any kind of frontline workers.
I'm talking to you!

We move forward with a plan, with intention, with heart.
We put a little—or a lot—
of thought, and energy,
into *the who we are* and *the who we want to be*.

And, by our own doing, we become.
We strive. We accomplish.
We use our God-given gifts to move forward in life,
on track—on point—on goal.

And most especially, we do so,
with God-with-us as our helper—
present to us as our teammate, our coach and our friend—
beside us, encouraging us,
in every step of the way. Amen.

ON BEING A BYSTANDER IN OUR OWN LIVES

There are many ways to describe our lives,
and our approaches-to-life-as-we-know-it.
"Life Journey," "Adventure and Odyssean Living,"
"Purpose-Driven Life," "Holy Living,"
"Abundant Living" . . . even "Come What May."

These are all action-based terms,
inferring that the individual is actively or even pro-actively
doing, or being, or perceiving, or living out a certain quality of life
that is integral to their well-being
or to their chosen or preferred lifestyle.

I heard a remark recently, that it is sad,
and downright difficult to acknowledge,
that being a bystander in one's own life
is a bitter and ugly reality,
and, that sadly, being a bystander in one's own life,
is a bitter reality for most.

Just simply watching life go on all around us,
and living on the periphery,
and "being there" only subtly and superficially,
without questioning or striking up a cause,
or not even having a sense of purpose
or a say in the direction of life,
makes us reflect deeply
on what is actually driving our own life
and fueling our daily living.

Two iconic songs of the wind—from Dylan in the 1960's
and from Kansas in the 1970's—drift into mind here.
"Life Blows On" could be a new original track.
In these simple lyrical laments,
we can truly be bystanders in our own lives,
and in all life.
Uncommitted. Uninvolved.
Uninspired. Unimpassioned.

I recall a punch-line story about God's will in our lives.
A paddler in a canoe, on a wilderness wild whitewater rivercourse,
was simply allowing the canoe
to cruise over the crests of the high-water rapids,
fully trusting that God would lead him and keep him safe.

He was unknowingly approaching a massive waterfall
when a voice in his head called out loudly . . .

"I WILL keep you safe, *but you have to put your paddle in the water!*"

I believe with my whole heart,
that unless we want to be contented
with being everyday bystanders in our own lives,
we must put our paddles in the water!

We must have visions—set goals and take actions—
which lead us into wholesome living,
and which carry us into lives befitting
our goals and our gifts.

We must paddle, swim, and dance toward the goal, toward the Light,
with a certain joy and energy and vitality,
bringing us off the sidelines and out of the spectator galleries
and into the very heartbeat of life itself.

We might make mistakes. We may stray off the path.
We might possibly find other way-more-exciting-and-challenging,
and meaningful paths along the way!
But, we must be the protagonist-not-the-bystander
in our own unfolding story.
We must be actually-present-and-actively-engaging.
We must not be merely spectators
or passive observers.

May we truly live out our own story,
attuning to the still small voice within—listening to the Sacred,
to the Sound of the Eternal—
all the while vowing
to keep our paddles planted firmly
in the swift-moving waters of life. Amen.

STAND UP AND SLAM—SLAM POETRY!

Muster your courage and find your voice.
Not your quiet poet voice.
Slam your way into the hearts of an eager audience,
and stir them into action.
Have no regrets in voicing your truths.

Draw on your passion, and your conviction.
Speak the outrage that disturbs your soul.
Articulate your emotions and speak in images—
in vibrant colours and in vibes.
Let your words arise—
at once pervasive as a mushroom cloud,
and, as healing as the 23rd Psalm.

Be the voice of today, and of tomorrow.
Be the encouragement and the energy for others
to live out all of their unfolding stories
with hope, with peace, with purpose,
with justice—with compassion and love.

May you find the courage and the resolve, to
speak your heart, speak your truth, speak your truths.
Stand up and slam. Now is the time to be heard.
I'm talking to you! Amen.

IN LOVE, LET US ALL SPEAK OUR TRUTHS

Truth softly spoken is humane.
  Truth withheld is untruth.
    Truth-telling is a must.
      Whole truth—no omissions—is imperative.
        Timely truth is essential. Critical.

For what?
  For everything!

For integrity and grace.
  For transparency.
    For clarity.
      For just getting it right.
        For complete-thoughtful-thorough communication.
          For sensitivity and consideration.
            For peace of mind.
              For goodness and for humanity.

Let us all be open and honest.
  As hard as it is to do, let us all speak our truths.
    "Beauty is truth, truth beauty."[5]
      Let us all rise up together,
        in respect and honor,
          in love and compassion, in community.
            Let us embody love. Speak love.

5. John Keats, "Ode on a Grecian Urn" in *Annals of Fine Arts for 1820*, 638.

And then, in love,
  let us all speak our whole and timely truth.
    Amen.

SOMETHING SEEMS SOMEWHAT OFF . . .

Covid 19 has created many unprecedented
health and social and economic imbalances,
and it takes astute minds and timely critical thinking
to weigh all of these forces, and to understand
their impacts on our personal lives
and in our daily living.

It also takes individual self-reflective practice
and the focused interior work of discernment
to bring Light into this cloud of shadows and darkness—
into this globally imposed solitary existence—
into this unhealthy-realm-
of-seeming-disconnect-and-
perceived-aloneness-in-our-
strange-new-wilderness.

On a deeply personal level, in the isolating world of Covid,
our own uniquely inherent matrix of integrity and wholeness,
can be sensed as unraveling,
as becoming unglued, as diminishing—
as being whittled away
and randomly scattered in the wind.

Body mind and spirit become fragile,
enduring veritably long nights of estrangement,
and an unwelcomed sense of separation.

In attempting to reconcile this dark and ominous reality,
we begin to ask ourselves the questions . . .

"What is my integrity built on?," and
"What makes me whole?," and
"What do I need to do, to overcome this precarious
leaning-Tower-of-Pisa-feeling,
before I actually crumble, tumble,
and fall down hard?"

And this is where our individual differences come into play.
There is no one answer. There is no right answer.

The Light of understanding might dimly start to shine
as we simply begin to reflect on our worrisome state of being.

We may begin to ask
"Are we failing to trust in our leaders, in ourselves, in our God?!"
"Are we allowing fear to lead us, rather than love?"
"Are we wrongfully believing
that our precious-internal-wholeness-and-integrity-matrix
is built upon our layered foundations
of social, financial, and economic relations?"

"Is our "disconnect" and perceived isolation
from the rapid-fire-interconnected-life-as-we-knew-it,
truly a bad thing?"

"What is the glue, the true glue, that holds us together,
and keeps us moving—
forward, upright, strong and contented?"

It is in the very asking of these questions,
and in listening deeply to discern the answers,
and in attuning to the Presence of God in our lives,
that we discover our deeper-most glue,
our true glue—our deepest Sacred connectedness.

And once we can actually feel the bonding,
the stickiness and the steadfastness of this glue,
we no longer sense that we are leaning, crumbling, tumbling—
being whittled away, breaking or broken.
We are grounded, safe, secure—no matter what.

We are gathered-in, collected, held-fast and strengthened,
simply by being in relationship with "God-with-us."
We are NOT excluded and isolated,
rather, we feel included and "together,"
and refreshingly whole.

Our own knowing and embodying "God-with-us" is our glue.
We may not have, or ever have, all of the Covid answers,
but, in living out this very truth, "God-with-us,"
we are not isolated, or separated and somewhat "off,"
rather we are whole, one, and totally "on"!

Let us find strength and purpose,
and contentment,
in knowing "God-with-us." Amen.

ALONE

"Alone"
can be a very real presence of mind,
or state of being,
or reality of life,
but never, ever,
is it a state of faith in God—
Emanuel—
God-with-us.

Thanks be to God,
that we are never, ever, ever, truly alone. Amen.

ARE WE ASKING THE RIGHT QUESTIONS?

Are we asking the right questions?

Oftentimes, our musings lead us to answers, new Light, new truths.

But, still we wrestle.
  The answers we come up with,
    are as uncomfortable as the questions that preceded them.

And we sit with these answers—and our discomforts—
  and invariably we get stuck there.

Then bad things happen.
  We resent. We internalize and make it personal.
    We get defensive. We rationalize.
      We ask Why? And we dwell on the Why.

We ourselves start to unravel
  with doubts, insecurities, wishful thinking, and what-ifs.
    We spiral down, down, down.
      Darkness lurks.

Enough already. Break the cycle! Now!

Don't like the question?
  Ask a different question!
    Ask a better question!
      Ask the right question!
        Ask someone else!
          Ask God!

Then trust
that the answer IS out there—
that the truth IS out there—
that the Light IS out there.

Trust that with your own contemplative approach,
you can get past the darkness and step into the Light,
by asking the right questions.

Trust that with your own convictions,
you CAN find an acceptable and workable answer,
and move forward.

Get unstuck!!! Unstuck yourself!!!
Ask the right question, and then, truly listen for the answer.

Through trust, there is hope.
Through hope, there is Light.
Through Light, there is truth. Amen.

ASK BETTER QUESTIONS

Sometimes when we ask a question, we simply do not like the answer.
In our ordered lives, with our needs for completeness of understanding—
in our own reactive ways—
we continue to seek other answers—
hopefully better answers—
easier-to-swallow answers.

Or, perhaps, there is no answer—
no possible or plausible answer—to our question.
The answer does not exist.
This most certainly does not sit well with us seekers.

On that note,
we rise in anger, clouds of frustration swirl, and tension mounts.
A vicious cycle of unrequited questioning—
of perpetual angst—of internal unrest—
settles into our midst,
creating disillusionment and disorder.

We can stop this cycle of cumulative chaos.
We can simply use our brains and our astute powers of perception,
to retrace our steps to examine fully,
the situation in all its complexity and minutiae of details.

Then, with our new insights and perspectives,
we can reframe the facts and comprehend them
on a different or deeper level.
Then truly, we can ask better questions.

When we ask better questions,
there's every chance for truth to emerge,
and for actionable answers to follow—
answers that lead to actions,
that lead to change,
that will lead to new outcomes,
new questions, and new answers.
All we need to do,
is slow down,
and ask better questions.

Dear God, help me to see. Truly see.
Help me to notice, perceive, and understand,
with my ever truth-seeking heart,
that my subsequent questions will be better questions,
that the right and good answers
indeed can be found. Amen.

THERE WILL ALWAYS BE TOADS

The toad is not hurting anyone.
  The toad is just being a toad.
    It is living its life, hopefully its best life.
      Just let it be.

The toad hopped into your space for a time,
  into your life for a moment,
    freely, with grace.
      No agenda. No ulterior motive.
        Just let it be.

The toad stopped in its tracks
  and looked up and stared at you.
    In fear? In trust? In awe? In envy?
      It didn't bark or bite or sting or even mess up.
        Just let it be.

The toad stayed awhile, taking its place in your space—
  watching, learning, knowing, growing.
    Then, it moved away. Moved on. Slowly. Surely.
      Just let it be.

There will always be toads, in our lives, on our paths.
  They come for a season, a reason, or not. Just let them be.

Dear God, May we all, just let them be. Amen.

FREE FLOW—MAY THIS BE SO!

Service. Compassion. Love.
  These all have one thing in common.
    They are given freely.

If service is not given freely, it's called obligation.
  If compassion is not given freely,
    it is dis-ingenuous-ness, or hypocrisy.
      If love is not given freely,
        it clearly isn't love to begin with.

There's nursing care, and then, there's a caring nurse.
  Nursing care can in truth, be delivered by an uncaring nurse.
    The difference is made by the nurse's heart, i.e.,

He/she has a servant heart, or not.
  He/she approaches all patients with compassion, or not.
    He/she leads with love, or not.

My eyes were opened over my thirty-three year nursing career.
  In my naivety,
    I thought all nurses entered the profession
      because they cared.
        Wrong.

I quickly learned that burn-out was a thing—a really big thing—
  that some nurses' hearts were wholly jaded
    by government politics, and hospital politics,
      by life-experience and, by love-experience.

A nurse who was not raised in a home filled
with free-flowing service, love and compassion,
who has never witnessed a servant-heart
giving their all—daily—in love and compassion,
who doesn't intrinsically know the joy of
giving-of-self-to-others,
who only knows how to self-preservationally
set boundaries to protect
themselves and their own heart . . .

this nurse can fall short in caring for their patients.
Not to say that they cannot learn all of this—for they can!

A nurse who intuitively knows—
who intuitively knows how to care—
who intuitively knows that
care changes things in a really big way,
this nurse will most definitely
make a difference in the lives of many.

Nurses who feel put upon, or hard done by,
or burdened in giving nursing care—
these nurses need to find another career.

Their heart is not in their work.
They are clearly not called to serve.
They are not called to reach out with compassion and love.

And now in reflecting on my own nursing career,
I see just how toxic the nursing environment was.

It rocks me—it rattles me deeply—
in remembering some of the harsh comments
that some nurses made to their patients,
and to each other.

Their hearts had hardened.
There was no glimmer or shimmer of service in their approach.
There was no compassion or love—
these were replaced by coldness, contempt,
and need for control.

They were nurses who repeatedly hurt their colleagues,
emotionally hurt them,
and quite frankly,
they hurt their patients too.

All patients need to be served, by a nurse with a servant heart.
All patients deserve respect and compassion,
no matter their circumstance or place in the world.
All patients should know and feel
that their nurses are leading with love.

In context, in the big picture, in a perfect world,
caring comes from the heart.
And a heart full of compassion and love
is truly a servant heart.
A heart that is free to serve
with love and compassion
is the ultimate quality of a caring nurse.

May we all, not just nurses, look inward at our hearts.
May we reflect on what flows freely, or not,
from our hearts to the world around us.

And then, may we take steps to open our hearts into a free-flow.
May we emerge from our deepest reflections,
with servant hearts—each and every one of us.
May this be so. Amen.

INTO THE DEPTHS OF THE DIRT

Life is not always going to be "life on our terms."
It can be unclean, unkempt, unpolished, unfinished.
It can be sourly and bitterly distasteful.
Even nauseating.

But the wise and strong,
the compassionate and respectful,
the upright and honorable—the empaths—
they know how to deal with dirt.

Rather than distancing themselves
and walking away from it—tiptoeing around it—
or quietly sweeping it under a carpet,
or demonstratively spitting on it
while regarding it as lower—lowly—
they take it
and look at it more closely.

They attempt to see it more clearly,
to know the ground that it sits upon, to know its original source,
and to feel its merit and its movement,
and its place in the world.

They cease to be reactive, judgmental and fearful.
They then discover, and come to acknowledge,
the direction of the dirt, the perspective of the dirt,
the finery of the dirt,
and the soul of the dirt.

They see the dirt in the Light.
They can even speak to—and speak for—the dirt.
They hold the dirt close,
with the loving arms of humanity,
and the big strong arms of understanding.

When dirt is in our lives,
the communal-collective-wider-we
must be responsible, and accountable.
We need to rise up with integrity
to embrace the dirt, honor it,
and be present to it.

For we are all the same—we are all made of dirt—
earthy, grungy dust and dirt—
and to dirt we shall all return.
Life is way, way, way too short to disregard the dirt.
Let us all incline ourselves—
willingly and intentionally.
Let us all lower ourselves—
into the depths of the dirt. Selah
Amen.

RELEASED—LOADS LIFTED

The load is only heavy when we carry it—
  when we allow ourselves to be burdened by it.

We carry things way, way, way too long.
  For all the wrong reasons . . .

Unforgiveness. Contempt. Hurt.
  Lack of clarity leading to misunderstanding and mistrust.
    Indecisiveness.
      Lack of courage to work things out.
        Fear of speaking truth.
          Fear of showing vulnerability.
            Pride. Silly human pride.

The very minute we drop it, or let it go,
  we are released, relieved, renewed. Reborn.

We immediately sense a freshness, a newness,
  a lightness, a brightness, everywhere.
    Inside and out.

We sense a new pathway toward whole-person-wholeness.
  A sense of being no longer lost, but found.
    A sense of rebirth, of opening self—
      of inner growth and transformation.
        Out with the old and in with the new.

An energized spirit arising.
  A return to a balanced well-being.
    A welcomed return to original self.

A change that is deeper, greater,
  more healing and more personally affirming
    than any pithy utterance in mantra—
      in word or song, or prayer.

Let us know the loads we carry.
  Let us understand them, acknowledge them,
    and put them in their right place—in perspective.

Then, at the right time, let us release them!
  May we with intention, let them go!
    May we move onward in peace, in contentment, in hope.
      May this be so. Amen.

WET IS WET

Wet is wet.
When you're not wet, you're dry.
Can't be just a little bit pregnant, or a little bit married.
You either are, or you aren't.

Can't be just a little bit obese.
You CAN be a little bit fat, but, obese is clearly obese.
Obese means obese. End of story.

Hurt is hurt.
You might not be able to see hurt,
or even tell that someone is hurting,
but to that person, hurt is hurt.
Not a little bit hurt, or somewhat hurt.
Hurting is physical,
emotional or spiritual,
or, all of these at once.
Black and white.
Here and now.
Hurt is hurt. Ouch.

May we all come to recognize
the hurts, the hurt, and the hurting.
May we be able to see with our hearts,
and know and feel, the hurt.

May we rise up to be there,
to share with those who are hurting,
to care for the hurting,
to begin the journey into healing, with the hurting.

Thanks be to God who knows the hurts, the hurt, and the hurting,
who walks with those who are hurting,
who knows hurt, like we do.

We all need God to weep with us.
May God know the wetness of our tears.
Wet is wet. Hurt is hurt. God is God.
And then, may God dry our tears. Amen.

LET'S HUMAN WELL

Reaching out with understanding.
Reaching out with compassion.
Reaching out with love.
This is humane. This is human. This is humanity.

"Love your neighbor as yourself."
"Do for others as you would have others do for you."
"If they slap you in the face, turn the other cheek." "Forgive."
"The best things in life are not things."
"Seek your treasures in heaven, not here on earth."
"Everything, everyone, all life and being,
is made of God,
and therefore is Holy, Sacred."

We were taught these things.
We know these things.
We intuit these things.
We take these to heart and we internalize them.

But, others who are sadly mal-aligned
to power, authority and control—to evil—
have forgotten these teachings,
these words of wisdom,
this honorable way of life.

The shadows of their greed and their lust fall upon our hearts.
We feel hopeless, even desperate, in hearing ongoing news of
the war zones and malevolence of Rwanda,
Eritrea, Nicaragua, Afghanistan, Syria, Ukraine,
Israel and Palestine—
they cloud and darken our hearts.

The unrest, fear and chaos
arising in the aftermath of US border and territorial threats—
all of this disturbs us deeply, disheartening all of us.

We are heart-sick in their sin-sick ways.
Communism-Fascism lures, limits, lurks.
Our spirits sink down low,
as we witness the atrocities, the inhumanities,
the war crimes, and the oppressive ways.

We vowed as a world in 1945, "No More War!"
And collectively, this we must do again. All of us.
We must human well. We must human better. All of us.
We must gather our voices together. Stronger together.

Our voices must be heard, and understood.
Our prayers must be spoken, lifted up.
Our convictions must rise up for all to see—
for all to live by and be—at peace.

Let us all strengthen our resolve and our conviction
to seek peace, and justice, in this war-crazed world.

Let's take genocide and supremacy and hatred out of our vocabulary,
and let us hold fast to our own wholesome teachings and visions,
of universal respect and compassion and love.
And peace.

Let all of the world leaders embrace humanity,
lead with integrity, lead with grace.
No one wins through war. No one.

Let us all return to basics.
Let's be human.
To do anything less than this,
is a shameful crime against humanity.
Let us not be criminal.
Let's human right.
Let's human better.
Let's human well. Amen.

AT THE RIGHT TIME

It is my hope that a little wisdom, truth and Light
is shimmering—shining—through these words . . .

I like to use the phrase "At the right time."
I use it a lot!

In my perpetual glass-half-full approach,
in my engaged living, in my wholehearted life,
I do look forward to things which are
conceptual and top-of-mind today—
to things that will most certainly become
part of my reality—our reality—
down the road—at the right time.

For example, the proposed and highly anticipated teatime with a friend
gets written into my daily Day-timer—into my agenda—
at the right time.

The promise to bring a concept into reality
actually begins with naming a plan, a place,
a team and a leader, resources—and a start date—
all, at the right time.

The intense long-term project
finally has a firm and committed completion date,
at the right time.

The right time is nebulous, until it is not.
The right time is only a whim, until it actually appears.
The right time is as real as it needs to be.
The right time, happens, at the right time.

May all of our promises, plans, visions, goals and dreams emerge,
at the right time.
May we all find our way,
at the right time.
May God of all our hearts help us to know,
the right time. Amen.

AFFIRMATION

BURST

Bursting through the quiet, the calm, the night—
 came the joy, the fire, the Light—
  stirring, awakening, befriending,
   in the very depths of my soul.

I've come alive. I'm stepping up. I stand in awe.
 My heart is love. I am love. I am Light.

I've drifted. I've sifted and shifted.
 And now, I'm Godly-gifted.

God's grace is upon me, like the waters of the grandest waterfall—
 hurtling, barreling, and soaring over the escarpment ledge—
  to grace the river below.
   Yes! Grace is used intentionally twice—
    as both a noun and a verb—
     in the same insightful sentence!!!

I am the River. I am the Light. I am the Love.
 I am open and flowing and free—I'm ready to receive—
  I am blessed, indeed.

Oh God of Holy Lovelight, burst away, and fill me, I pray. Amen.

LIGHT

My true north, my guiding star,
my orbits, my pathways, my purpose,
the ripples of my passion, my echoes, my music,
my mirror reflections,
my inferential words,
my curling and curving poesy—
all have one thing in common.

Light.
Holy Light.
The Holy Lovelight of God.
The Holy Emanant Light of me.

God of Holy Lovelight,
help me, allow me, enable me,
to shine brightly,
in Your Light, in my own Light,
together as one Light. Amen.

SHIMMERINGS, SHININGS, AND SPARKLES

Wise ones once said:

"Happiness is homemade."
  "No one can bring you inner happiness, peace, and joy, but you.
    Happiness starts with you."

"Don't let other people bring you down, put you down, tear you down.
  Illegitimi non caborundum.
    You know who you are, and whose you are.
      Let your Light shine brightly from within."

"Only you know how to make your heart smile.
  Figure out how to make your heart smile
    broadly, openly, freely, daily,
      here and now,
        now and always."

I am but the summation
  of my life experiences, my life learnings, my life stories.
    I have been shaped and shaded,
      by much and by many.

But it is the shining and the shimmering and the sparkles from within
  that have truly formed me the most.
    I am contented. I am free to be me.
      I am Light. Thanks be to God. Amen.

WHO DO I WANT TO BE?

Well, first of all, who do I NOT want to be?!

Negative, pessimistic, angry,
full of contempt and spite and vengeance,
controlling, demanding, demeaning, dehumanizing,
unaware, uninformed, unrealistic,
closed-minded or blind,
needy, self-centered, and self-focused.

Please please please, nudge me, and call me out on it,
if you sense any of this in me. I mean it!
I am not—and I never want to be—
that person.

I look up to all of my close family members,
and I see qualities that stir me,
inspire me, connect me, and motivate me.
I strive to embody—emulate—
these exemplary and wholesome ways of my people.
I do strive to form myself, in their ways.

Dad—strong, clear thinking, prepared, energetic,
unafraid of speaking his truth.
Mom—ultra-creative, practical.
My sister BJ—humanly insightful, selfless, joyful.
Nana Rennie—loving, nurturing,
compassionate, generous of self.

Grampie Chester—hardy, persevering, driven.
Nana Rose—calm, gracious, attentive listener.
Grandpops David—poet, focused, content.

And this is just the beginning.
Self-knowing.
Knowing who I want to be.

All of the rest simply falls into place—
it becomes my pathway, my journey,
as I live out my life, slowly becoming my desired-self,
gradually shaping and forming myself—
body mind and spirit—
into the who—into the whom I want to be—
into the one I want to become.

May I always have a larger-than-life-sense of who I am,
and who I want to be.
May God ever gift me with this knowing,
with this perception,
with this understanding
of me and my place in the world. Amen.

HERE I STAND

Here I stand, in the moment, in the now.
  Calm. Centered. At peace.

But, I wasn't always "here."
  I wasn't always present.
    I wasn't always so chill.

My centeredness truly evolved.
  It took intention and focus
    and a great deal of fine-tuning of my own self-awareness.

I had to learn what it meant to be present,
  to be in the moment. To live in the moment.
    To attune deeply to my here and now.
      To know my now.

And "here" is a beautiful place.
  "Here and now" is even more beautiful.
    Present, focused, aware, contented, complete.

"Here I stand" is an utterance of self,
  an offering of self in time and in place.
    "Here I stand" is conviction, awareness, and knowing,
      all wrapped up in a pretty package of presence.

Here. Now. Me. One. Here I stand. Thanks be to God. Amen.

I BELONG . . .

I belong . . .

to a wonderful world,
  worthy of my wonderment and my wanderlust.

to an ancience—to an ancient-ness—in ancestry and culture—
  that calls down through eternity to my very soul.

to a family who loves me,
  unconditionally.

to a community
  which I love to serve.

to a church
  that nourishes me and nurtures me.

to a faith
  that strengthens me, comforts me,
    and forms me daily on my journey.

to a spirituality
  which is grounded in the ancient Celtic Wisdom,
    and, in the Sacred.

to God,
  who calls me by my name,
    who calls me to serve with love,
      who loves me with a Father's heart.

Belonging is beautiful.
I am filled up with a sense of true belonging,
and I am well on my way to becoming complete,
to being whole,
to being at peace.

May we all find our way in this world,
knowing we belong,
knowing that we are part of something bigger,
knowing a connectedness that veritably binds.

May we find hope and assurance,
in this knowing. Amen.

COLOR ME BLESSED

Color me 'part of'—
one-with, integral, connected, interconnected,
mosaic, spiral, fractal, order, chaos.
New and fresh. Ancient, yet in season.
Tender, yet tough. Frail and fine.

Isn't it a grand perceptual awakening
to attune to the interconnectedness of all—
from microcosm to macrocosm—
from particulate to cosmic—
from Human to Divine?!

Isn't it wonderfully freeing, to revel in and to reverence
the interconnectedness of all?!

Isn't it Holy, Divine, Sacred,
to witness the mystery and the wonder,
of all parts of the whole—
of all interconnectedness—
and to simply let them be—Mystery?!

Might we all open our hearts
to the wonder and the mystery
of all that links us together—
of all that connects us to God—
of all that connects us in life,
and in love, and in Light?

Color me driven—
    at work, in the pool, on the field, academically—
        always with a raging hunger and thirst,
            to get things right.

Isn't it just so very energizing to stride out,
    with both eyes—and with heart and mind—
        clearly focused on the target?
            Forward, onward, on point!

Isn't it fulfilling, gratifying, enriching,
    to cross the cherished finish line
        knowing that you had put your whole self out there
            and you went the distance—and the extra mile?

Might we all simply strive, and drive ourselves,
    to work hard, to dream big, to get it right, to soar?

Color me kind—
    compassionate in the ER, and on the street,
        and in the darkened places where very few would even go.

Isn't it just the right thing to do,
    to instinctively reach out, to encourage, to support,
        to be present to, to give, to share—
            with all of those who, in their time of need,
                would never ask for the help
                    that they so clearly and desperately need?

Isn't it heartwarming to know in your heart
    that your timely, small act of kindness,
        generosity or compassion, just made a huge world of difference
            to one darkened soul?

Might we all embody these exquisite words—
    all souls matter?

Color my servant heart—
in body mind and spirit wholeness,
as I walk alongside, prayerful and peaceful.

Isn't it a true calling from deep within, to step forward to serve?
Isn't it the gist of the story—the central appeal—
in the parable of the Good Samaritan,
to go out of our way and then some,
to serve both neighbors and strangers alike
with a willing servant-heart?

Might we all take up the Scriptures and carry them in our hearts,
arise and shine—and serve?

Color me deep—
contemplative, attuned,
in the moment, here and now, present.

Isn't it an expansive and spacious place to be,
aware, attending, taking in, sensing, absorbing,
wondering, questioning, querying—simply being?

Isn't it awesome—stirring and moving—
to take the time to enter into the depths,
to deep dive into a deeper well of wisdom,
to dwell there, to be nurtured by appreciative wonder,
to be momentarily caught up in—
or even lost in—the contemplative realm?

Might we all take a moment and enter in,
and listen for the Light of my words?

Color me whole—
centered, contented, strong in my faith,
whole, yet part of something so much bigger than my single self.

Isn't it absolutely completing, knowing that you are ever and always
befriended and beloved by God?
In your wholeness, you become one-with-God!

Isn't it simply mysterious, and mystical, in understanding
that you are OF God,
that you are Light,
that you are Sacred?

Might we all take a breath, and take all of these colors into our souls—
might we all breathe in all of these colors—
might we all make these colors our very own—
make them come alive in our colorful wholehearted lives?
We might then sigh, and speak these words,
blissed be, blessed be!

Color me blessed—
color me humble—
color me grateful—
thanks be to God! Amen!

LET'S TALK, LET'S LISTEN

Conversation is sharing.
Sharing of story, emotion, facts, wisdom,
perspectives, reality and dreams.

Conversation involves listening, exploring ideas, working things out.
Understanding. Unloading and venting. Unpacking.
Asking. Supporting. Encouraging.
And so much more.

Conversations can be superficial or deep.
They can carry a tone—
sarcasm, judgment, anger
versus empathy, hope and love.

The tone can be overbearing, or barely there, or hidden.
Sometimes mixed and confusing . . .

And oftentimes, the dominant perceived tone
can be very distracting . . . Hmmmmm . . .

Conversations can be focused, targeted, mission-directed,
or, scattered, free and wanderlusting.
These latter conversations are the very best kind!!!
Follow the agenda, or, follow your nose!

BUT, ENOUGH ALREADY!!! Here begins the real message . . .

I long for meaningful conversation.
I live for stirring conversation.
Deep conversation that takes us "somewhere."
Profound conversation that energizes and incites,
as well as disturbs and opens eyes.

Conversation that affirms and elevates and inspires.
This does not necessarily mean intellectual conversation. But it can.

I long to go deep, to go deep in conversation
with a friend or with a stranger,
to go deep knowing that someone
is walking right there with me into the depths,
and isn't desperately trying to run away
or return to the surface for fresh air.

Walk with me in conversation! Come with me!
Leave sarcasm and holier-than-thou-one-upmanship at the door.

Let's talk. Let's share. Let's truly listen.
Listen deeply for what body mind and spirit need to hear, and to say.
Let's listen for the Sacred—
in our conversation, in our hearts, in our midst.

I'm so ready. I'm so open.
Let's talk about what really matters, here, now, this.
God will be with us, for sure. Amen.

PERHAPS . . .

Perhaps I'm from another place, another time—
maybe even another realm.
Sometimes I feel very alone
in my ways, in my ideals, in my very way of being.

At all times, I seek peace.
I love unconditionally.
I take time to be.
To simply be.

I'm not wanting to get caught up in busy-ness,
or to have negative energies spent
on petty and insignificant things.
I'm free. I'm me.

I'm pleased and blessed to lead a simple life based on
simple truths,
simple rules,
simple kindnesses.
Simplicity implicitly.

I choose my path. I choose my stresses.
I choose peace and hope and joy and love,
over chaos, fear, pain and loneliness.

I choose faith—faith in God who is ever-present to me.
I choose an intimate relationship with God
who knows my heart—who loves me, with a Father's heart.

I love who I am,
  whose I am,
    where I'm from,
      and where I'm going.

I'm present, in the here and now.
  I am whole.
    I am me.
      God is with me. Amen.

May I always and ever, be comfortable with who I am.

May I know in my heart that there are indeed
  others out there like me, who strive to live out their lives,
    according to their beliefs,
      according to their faith,
        according to their own truths,
          led by their Light within,
            ever-listening to the drumbeat of their soul—
              ever-arising to the call from deep within.
                Amen.

I WISH . . . .

Dreams are dreams, day or night.
  Visions are visions, filled with hope and insight.

But wishes? Wow!
  They are random and spontaneous and fleeting.
    Often, they are not well thought out.
      But then again, wishes do arise from
        our deepest depths.

It is this "latter wishing" of which I speak.
  Heartfelt. Profound. Visceral.
    From the very depths, of me.

I wish . . . .

That the world could hold up humanity, first and foremost.
  Love, compassion and respect for all would freely abound.

That love, and only love, would drive every human thought and action.

That wars could end, and that world leaders' hunger and greed
  for dominion, power, authority and control would cease.

That "this hunger" be replaced by a hunger to love and to share,
  and to serve—to serve well—
    for the common good, the greater good—
      for the shared vision
        of being best possible stewards of the earth.

That all peoples could TRULY SEE humankind
as one brotherhood, one sisterhood, one family,
to be honored, cherished, protected and upheld.

My wish, in a nutshell,
is that all humankind embody human-kindness—
that all humankind could human better—human well—
human now.

My wishes are grand, and I am small. Just me.
One voice. Mine
One Light. Mine.
One wish. Mine.

But, as one tiny candle can light up a whole room,
so too may I wish that my wishes,
can light up humankind.
So be it. May it be so. Amen.

"BEST" IS A FOUR LETTER WORD

"Best in the World," "Best in Class," "Best All Round."
Great titles for the competitive world.
Even great terms for the business world,
the engineering world, and the world of IT.

"Best" drives productivity, and the economy—and greed.
It is a prime motivator in research and development.
"Best" and "First" and "Leading Edge" are all BFF's—
best friends forever, in the first world of progress.

But, in my heart, in my life, in the moment, "Best" is meaningless.

Yes, doing my best, doing the best I can, and being the best I can be,
are all softer sounding, and perhaps easier to embody.

"Best" connotes ranks, judgments, and better-thans.
In my individual and in our collective desires to be human,
and to human well,
we must not compete.
We must not strive to outshine,
or outdo the other,
or out-be, in the other's eyes.
It doesn't matter.

Being the best in humanity, for humanity, among humanity,
really doesn't matter.

Being human, living out my life with care and concern for the other,
with respect and compassion, and with love—this truly matters.
Being human is simply that—being human.

No best. No first. No score. No rank. No better-than.
Simply being human is my want, my will, my way.

Being more fully human, and becoming most fully human—
people write whole books about this.
I did too.

Becoming most fully human is not about
becoming extraordinary, outstanding,
phenomenal, or even superhuman.
It is not about being best.

Rather, it is truly the art and the passion
of becoming deeply, intensely, human.
It is a process towards actualizing my own humanity.
It is forward intentional movement
toward my own self-actualization
in all planes, in all realms, in all spheres.

I don't need, to be the best.
Never, ever, ever.

May I ever step up, step out, step forward,
with my Servant Heart,
with grace, with integrity,
and with the single desire to serve those in need.
May I feel most fully human, in so doing. Amen.

DRIVEN

I cling to what is right, and true, and good.
  Always and adamantly.
    And perhaps so, to a fault.

Please don't put words in my mouth!
  I did not say "I always need to be right"!
    But, in order for truth to be had by all,
      things must be said right, heard right,
        understood right, and done right.
          We all need *to just get it right.*

(My mother would simply cringe, shrivel up and shrink away, aghast,
  in response to my poetic bend of grammar here!)

My father was meticulous in all of his work—
  professionally, academically, and around the home.
    My mom's household was pristine—
      neat as a pin and totally organized.
        My nana's needlepoint and sewing
          were painstakingly perfect.
            My whole nursing career
              was framed by the "five rights."

Needless to say, my own "get-it-right-at-all-cost-approach" is a given,
  which I come by quite naturally.

The famous childhood fairy tale could truly be re-titled
  "Janis and the Pea"!

I am indeed driven by the right, the true, and the good.
Anything else makes me restless!
I wrestle and writhe—and I worm and I squirm—
until its fixed—until it's right!
And these, my guiding principles, have led me—
they've bent me and shaped me,
and they've made me, me.

They help me find my way, my true north.
They help me to see my path,
to wander safely from my path,
to return to my path,
find comfort on my path,
and most of all, to love my path.

And sometimes, in all truth, I do get it wrong.
All wrong. Totally wrong.
Way off in left field.
It is here, that I'm driven the most,
to correct it.
To get it right—not to be right—
to just get it right.

My ride, my journey, my passage here on earth
is full of impeccable trust, vision, insight and integrity,
as I strive—as I drive—
as I am driven—to get it right.
God is with me, befriending me,
in the driving of my life. Amen.

FINDING JANIS

In asking the question "Who am I?,"
  my brain sets off on so many interesting and intriguing tangents.

Mystically, I would self-define in the extravagant uniqueness of
  Curved Light, Pavo, and L'Arte.
    But sadly, only the Physics and Linguistics Scholars,
      and the elite Parfumeurs
        would pay attention
          to my illusive poetic metaphors.

Sigh. I wish to be so much more inclusive for my audience—
  more-identified-with and more relatable—
    and more human, and accessible.
      Please, please, please, bear with me!!!

From the perspective of the heart,
  I would identify with words
    like compassionate, selfless and loving.

Looking through the nebulous cloud of personhood,
  perhaps the words deep, intense, and focused
    would float to the top.

In the realm of all things social,
  the words "friendly-yet-introverted, and preferring one-on-one,"
    sum me up.

Through the lens of approach,
  open, optimistic, and occasionally opinionated.

In the veil of smoldering darkness, in the well of unspoken depths—
alone, misunderstood, full of doubt and innately paranoid.

In the light of wholeness, and in the abundance of grace,
I am blessed, beloved, gifted and graced.

Within the spiritual realm,
I am attuned, spacious, expansive,
and seeking the Sacred in all of life.
I am part of something big—
something far-far-greater-than myself.

In all things Holy,
I am born of original blessing,
born of essential goodness,
and born of the Holy Lovelight of God.
I am beloved.
I am Sacred.
I am Light.

In all matters, I am whole, centered, content, One.
And I am full of gratitude
for being one-with-God,
for being me,
for finally at last, finding Janis.
God knows, I wasn't always "found."

Curved Light, Pavo et L'Arte
Poetry, Peacocks and Perfume
Wisdom, Wonder and Whimsy—
All are Showings and Sparkles and Shimmers, of me!

Spend a moment, and dwell in your own depths,
and count up all of your colors,
and your curves,
and your complex-qualities-of-you.
Be playful. Be poignant. Be pithy.
Seek. Find. And give thanks.

In the fullness of the seasons, in the fullness of time,
in the fullness of Light, in the fullness of you,
find yourself, name yourself—
come to know and love yourself and give thanks. Amen.

LEAVING THE UN BEHIND

Unabashed, I will be me.
  I will strive to find myself, know myself, be myself,
    and most surely, love myself.

Yes, I'll become undone.
  Unleashed. Unrestrained. Unhinged.
    Uninhibited. Unbridled. Free.

I'm moving away from being unseen, unheard,
  unknown and misunderstood.

I'm rejecting old habits of feeling
  unwanted, unnecessary, unable.

Unforgiveness is not a cross that I presently bear.
  Maybe once upon a time I did,
    and maybe someday down the road I will again,
      but, not right now.

I am not defined by trends, contexts, movements, or times,
  or any other such external forces.

What I am and Who I am,
  are not defined by anyone, but me.
    And this is comforting to me.
      This is enlightenment.
        This, brings me deep deep peace.

Unrelenting, undaunted, I will move forward, onward,
in good time, in the right time.
It will be an unfamiliar path, for sure,
but with hope in my heart,
I am moving toward a new familiarity,
a new place, a new me.
I am more prepared,
I am more than ready for the journey.

The hidden will become un-hidden.
The unclear will become clear.
The unfinished me will continue to evolve,
on a path of self-awareness,
self-sufficiency and self-love.
The undetermined can be determined—
with me, through me, and by me.

My healing flows to me
like a river running through all of us, through all eternity,
like a river running gleefully down the slope to the sea,
like the waves out on the ocean,
approaching the distant shore—
perpetual, insistent, and welcomed.

Yup. The UN-world is no longer mine.
The intuition has risen.
The knowing has emerged.
The growing has begun.
The transcendence is truly mine.

And the power is all mine
to leave the UN behind me,
and to stand tall,
walking boldly forward in the Light,
to the Light.

For I am of the Light.
I am a Light-bringer.
I am a Light-bearing soul.

I am indeed, Light.
  God knows, I am Light.
    And to this I gratefully say, Amen!

DISCONNECTED

Here I am. Again.
  Alone with my thoughts.
    Alone with my energy.
      Alone with my creativity.
        Alone, but certainly not in any way, lonely.

In my deep well of creativity, I'm feeling a little drained.
  In my recent contemplative sits, I have
    examined, explored, analyzed, asserted,
      supported and contested, questioned and queried,
        reviewed, rejected and refuted, much.

In my ever-driven pursuit of wisdom, truth,
  knowledge-and-understanding, order, clarity and Light,
    I have grown. I have been shaped.
      I have been formed. I have become.

My head turns and my heart attunes—
  I am drawn into the depths
    of John Greenleaf Whittier's invitational truth . . .

"Drop thy still dews of quietness till all thy strivings cease.
  Take from our souls the strain and stress and
    let our ordered lives confess the beauty of thy peace,
      the beauty of thy peace."[6]

6. John Greenleaf Whittier, "The Brewing of Soma" in *The Atlantic Monthly April 1872 Issue*, page 389

I have been transformed on my journeys—on my quests—
in my silent sagacious sits.
My knowing is my growing.
My being and my seeing are so very freeing.
And transcendence has graced me—totally embraced me—
body mind and spirit.

I have a certain groundedness—a connectedness—
even an interconnectedness—
which makes me whole.

And my-being-whole
evokes a love, a peace, an unexplainable *joie de vivre*
which arises from deep, deep down in my soul.
Inlonracance indeed.

Every writer knows this. Every writer lives this.
And they too, live out these very questions . . . .

"If all is so darn well with me in my being,
in my becoming, and in my interior life,
why then, am I feeling so blatantly disconnected?"

"If I am so full, if I am so contented and at peace,
why do I feel so empty, or void of mattering?"

"If all is so truly right,
what is so wrong,
that I can find myself just sitting here, in the midst of all that is me,
and be drifting higher, farther, deeper—away, away, away . . .
attached to nothingness.
Airborne. Detached. Disconnected?"

There is no universal answer.
There is no tidy answer.
There is no right answer.

There is however, comfort in the knowledge,
  that in the reaches of my rambling,
    in the gift of my disconnect,
      in the freedom of my letting go,
        God is with me. Present to me.
          Gracing me. Connecting me.

Regrets? Salley Gardens?[7] Not!
  In the foggiest, and grey-ist of landscapes—
    in the most random and nebulous realms of my disconnect—
      God knows me, and holds me in His love—
        holds me in the Light.
          And to this I respond,
            in gratitude and in praise. Amen.

7. William Butler Yeats, "Down by the Salley Gardens" in *The Wanderings of Oisin and Other Poems*, 1889, un-numbered pages.

UNSPOKEN

Unspoken words.
Unspoken truths.
Unspoken love.
Unspoken pain.
Unspoken hell.

Unspoken how? Unspoken why?
How and why? Just like this . . .

Info withheld—to maintain privacy.
Details deferred—to a later date.
Story glossed over—
to minimize, or soften the blow, to shield or protect.
Facts omitted—to control the narrative.

My take?
Unspoken equals ugly.
Trust is thrown out the window.
Unspoken, cuts deeper
than a knife hot off the grindstone.
Leave it at that.
Let the unspoken be just that.
Unspoken.

Why? Because, whatever the unspoken is, cannot possibly hurt me
more than the unspoken-ness already has—already does.
I won't let it, anymore.

I've been shut out, one-time-too-many.
My turn. My bad. Now, I'm choosing the unspoken.
It's easier.
Not necessarily the right way.
It's just—simply—easier.

This conversation—this monologue—this soliloquy—this rant—is over.
Time to shut up and move on.
Feels good. Sooooo good.
I should have done this a long time ago.
I'm not here to hurt anyone.
I am now protecting me—and my heart.
Let the unspoken remain,
unspoken.

May I have the wisdom and insight,
the compassion and understanding, the diplomacy and the grace
to stand by my words—these words.
My broken heart needs to heal.

Unspoken is evil. Hurtful. Inexcusable.
May the unspoken remain unspoken—
let it hurt me no more.
I'm letting go of my hurting—
I'm sending evil packing. Amen.

I'M DONE

I usually give folks more chances than they deserve.
But, once I'm done, I'm done.

Perhaps I'm a pushover.
Or a doormat.
Or, I lack a backbone.

Not true at all, but folks do treat me as such.
They have for a really long time.
They feel good in taking advantage
of my very good-natured being,
and they assert their ways—they aggress.
They are driven by a deep-seated need,
to be in control, to maintain control,
and they prey on an easy target.

"Janis won't mind, she's pretty easygoing,
she won't stand in your way,
she won't complain. She's too nice to complain.
She'll let you walk all over her."

They are right, but only to a certain degree.
I don't stand up easily to bullies,
when my own needs are at stake.

But, in contrast, I do rise up to advocate for those
who cannot speak for themselves.
Aren't we all, a bit like this?
Maybe, a lot like this?!

But, today, I'm realizing,
that the control-hungry folks,
the bullies, and the mean-spirited—
they don't matter to me.
They just don't matter.
They have no power over me.

I've given them all so much space and time to witness my ways.
I've tried to shine, and lead by example,
to show them my ways
of respect and integrity, and compassion.

I've given of myself. I've tried to patch things up with honey.
And they are still driven to be in control.
They are still bullies. They are still mean-spirited.
They only know how to take, and not, how to give.

So, today, I'm done.
They've had their chances.
I have no need to change them, as they do not want to be changed.

Today, I'm letting go of any hope of healing,
of transformation, of reconciliation.
They can have their cold and controlling and tougher ways,
and, I'll go on being me.

I will go on, liking myself—liking who I am—liking who I've become—
full of grace, and peace, and gentleness of spirit.
I tried. I gave them so many chances.
I'm not apologizing.
I'm done.

Blessed are the peacemakers,
the salt of the earth,
the Lights of the world.
Blessed be me. Amen.

ON LETTING GO

Throughout our lives, we hold onto "things" that we value.
Property, possessions, friends, memories,
dreams, ideals, hopes and visions.
But things change, people change,
circumstances change, and times change.

And, as life is ever changing—ever curving—ever blurring—
we do let our "things" go. We choose to let them go.
Our "things" lose value, importance, priority—
they lose their sparkle and their color—
they cease to incite or inspire or engage
with any depth or meaning.
They may even begin to hurt us,
or limit us, or weigh us down.

"Excess baggage" it's called.
And we move on, forever changed by our "things."

We move on with gratitude for their impact
on our lives and on our personhood,
and on our hearts.

We move on, strengthened and empowered,
energized by their former presence in our lives.

We move on in peace,
knowing that whatever lies ahead
can be just as significant and beautiful and meaningful,
in our beholding hearts—in our beholding spirits.

We move on, from the comfort of the past,
through the reality of the present,
and onward into the challenges of the unknown future.
And we do all of this,
with integrity and resilience—
and trust.

We move on in grace, and in hope—
in awe and in wonder in the journey of life.
We value life and living,
and we value our God who made us all.

God the Creator makes,
and gives, and takes—
and loves us unconditionally,
and, this is one "thing" I can never, ever let go—
never, never, never.
I am loved.

In letting go of some "things"—
in choosing to let them go—
I stand tall—
I stand strong.

My heart is full.
I am truly blessed.
Above all "things" in life,
I want for nothing—
God makes me whole. Amen.

HOLDING ON TO ME

I am a positive person. I am a giver.
  Compassion comes easily for me,
    although my trust has always needed to be earned.

And I am a warm and open person,
  eager to share with strangers
    in tales and in story,
      in song and in sadness,
        in playfulness and deep conversation.
          I am who I am and I'm happy to be me.

And I think I will always "be me."
  I do not want any of this—any of me—to change.

But I AM changing. In a good way.
  I am becoming so much more self-aware and self-affirming.
    My deep knowing, my intuitive matrix,
      and my deep, deep faith
        are my superpowers.

As I am aging, I am becoming aware
  of people and times and powers that loom in the darkness.
    They may have the power
      or the urge or the will to shape me—
        to bend me or break me
          and even cut me to pieces.

And with my age, and wisdom, I know now, to not give them anything.
  Not my time as an audience, not my opinion—not even my energy.

I am learning to protect myself, to honor myself,
  to believe in myself, to love myself.

Why would I waste my energy on the words and actions
  of those who do not in turn
    protect me, honor me, believe in me and love me?
      Why? Why? Why?

I am strong—I am strengthened in my journey
  through my faith,
    through my knowing,
      through my powers of intuitive understanding.

I am a peacemaker
  and my own personal peace
    is just as important as any other cause.

This does not make me selfish
  in my self-preservational stance,
    or in my "strong-me" approach to life.

Rather, in protecting my inner peace,
  I am unequivocally better-equipped
    to face the world—
      to face the good and the bad and the downright ugly.

The mean-spirited, controlling, manipulative, arrogant,
  hot-mess, energy-draining monsters out there
    have absolutely no place
      in my heart or in my life or in my world.

I am me. Dear God, please let me be me.
Faults and all.
Kind, happy, generous,
open-hearted and wholehearted me.
Peaceful and peace-loving
and peace-seeking.
So be it. Amen.

I'M FREE

I'm free.
Finally freed at last.

I'm unburdened—unchained.
I'm unabashedly unbridled.

I've set myself free.
I've chosen to be free.
Free from nightmarish schedules, and oppressive rules.
Free from the North Star of perfection and control.
Free from the relentless haunts of
unspoken standards and codes, and,
from the niggle of nitpicking norms.

I'm relieved of the limitations set by ancient boundaries and walls—
of exclusive thinking and closed-minded judgmental prejudice.

Free to be me. Free to just be. Free to just be me.

Free to love and be loved.
Free to share in compassion—
openly, abundantly—
authentically.

Free to serve. Free to learn. Free to discern.
Free to stand up for whom and for what I believe in.
Free to speak up, speak out,
and to advocate for those who cannot.

Free to shape myself—spiritually, mystically, ethereally.
Free to become—free to become more/most fully human.
Free to really like who I am—
free to appreciate whom I am becoming.

Charlotte said it so well . . .
"I am no bird and no net ensnares me."[8]

I'm floating aloft,
caught up and carried away, on the bonnie breath of bliss.
Released of all cares.
Sailing, soaring, surfing—shining.
Cresting on a giganormous wave,
moving, planing, surging—
forward, onward, upward, inward—
freely.

How liberating! How lightening!
How lovely the view—the vista—
from the perspective of inner freedom.

Wholesome. Healing. Humbling.
Integrity in its absolute simplicity—
Integrity in its most luminous essence.

My heart delights, my soul is bright, my step is light—
in the favor and in the finery, and in the fervent fires of freedom.

I am delivered. Detached. Set free.
I'm free from all that insidiously harms me—
I'm free from all that invariably harms me.

May I ever be
undeniably, unconditionally, free. Me.
Thanks be! Amen!

8. Charlotte Brontë, in *Jane Eyre*, 338.

P-WORDS

Privileged? Maybe . . .
  Pretentious? Not!

I sleep in a comfortable bed every night,
  in a house that weathers all climates, all that nature sends its way,
    all seasons and storms.

I eat good food always,
  and it is readily available
    at quite a selection of nearby stores and markets.

I've had both a university and a college education,
  and I chose in my fifties,
    to return to school for a late career move
      into Parish Nursing Ministry.

I have now retired from a rewarding career,
  and I am living comfortably with a pension and securities
    which are both safe and protected.

I am loved. I have always been loved.
  I pray that I will always be loved.

My country is built on the cornerstone of democracy,
  and it stands strong in its protection of personal rights and freedoms.

We are a peace-keeping nation,
  and I am fortunate to live here in these times.

I have been privileged to be able to travel without restriction
(except during the Corona Virus Pandemic!)
in many countries—
large continents and tiny islands alike.

I've sampled the good life for sure—
spas and retreats, cultural events, religious studies,
and I've had a few really posh perk vacations,
courtesy of my husband's generous employers.

So, here comes the P-Word. Privileged.
Am I truly privileged? No.
This is just life as I know it—
as I've always known it in my first-world lived experience.
All of my needs are met, and more.
Dare I say, I think that privilege is seen and perceived
through the eyes of many and varied beholders.
Privilege is a blurry word with a capital B!

I don't consider myself privileged.
But, in the true meaning of the word, yes, I am privileged.
Shelter, food and water, love,
opportunities for education and employment—
all of these for me, are simply givens.

So are my human rights, personal freedoms,
and my rights to personal choices.

Indeed, by the textbook, I am privileged. And, I am so grateful.

But, I'll defend myself now,
against the modern and slurred version of the word "privileged."
I am not that person
who is pretentious, frivolous, entitled,
ungracious, ingenuous, or lofty.
Not me. Not never. Not ever.

With all of my "givens," comes my ever-present gratitude.
I am so fortunate—lucky—blessed—and honored,
to be living in my current here and now.

I will never, ever, take for granted
all of the work that generations before me have done,
and their visions and foresight,
that have brought me to my present way
of life and living and being—life as I know it.
No egocentricity here. My gratitude is overflowing.

And, my gratitude
coupled with my solid grounding in Jesus' teachings—
love thy neighbor (Good Samaritan), The Golden Rule,
seek peace, the last shall be first, salt and light—
all of these have perpetually stirred my servant heart
into choosing a lifetime of living the Compassionate Life—
in both my personal and my professional life.

My privilege,
WITHOUT my genuine gratitude and compassionate living,
might in effect, spell out some other bad P-Words.

But, my privilege DOES INDEED walk hand in hand
with my gratitude and my compassion—
it does call out loudly to me to use
my gifts, resources and connections,
and my knowledge,
to help those in need, those in want, those without.

To help those in the dark to reach up and reach out for the Light.
To bring Light into their darkness.
To encourage them to find the Light within.

My privilege is "the How" and my faith is "the How,"
in the "Who-What-Where-When-Why-and-How
equation of Christ-like living."
My love, my compassion,
can also be considered "the How."

Privileged? Yes!
Pretentious? No! Presumptuous? No! Prestigious? No!
Pleased to serve my God
with all of my gifts and with all of my heart? Yes!
Resounding Yes! Yes! Yes!!!

May I ever be grateful
for my privileges in life and living.
May I ever express my gratitude,
openly, freely, in earnest.

May I ever use my gifts, share my gifts,
and live out my faith,
to bring Light to the darkened world.

May I ever give thanks
to God for these gifts.
May I remain ever humble in heart,
and grateful in spirit,
in my faith journey,
in my Living Faith. Amen.

MY PEACE

"I do not need as the world needs.

My peace I give to me.
  At peace, I yearn to be.
    With my peace my heart is not troubled.

In my heart there are many chambers where my peace can dwell—
  in softness, in warmth, in the Light of my very being.
    I nurture my peace with my powers of positivity,
      with my love of life and living,
        and with the *joie de vivre* with which I was born."[9]

The slap of judgment, the lash of contempt, the wrath of arrogance,
  the bite of insensitivity, and the crush of mean-spiritedness—
    these all can literally bowl me over,
      and drop me to my knees, almost breaking me.

The weight of another person's angst and overwhelm,
  and their insidious hunger for control over me—
    these now weigh heavily on me, disturbing me deeply.

My peace is everything to me.
  And I am driven to protect it in my daily living.

9. Nuance of NRSV John 14: 27.

So, in my self-preservation mode,
in my woke insights and vision of true inner peace,
and my exquisite need for personal peace, I turn away.
And in so doing, I return to my peace.
My blessed peace.

I say goodbye to all that can hurt me and bring me down.
I bid farewell to all the hurtful and hateful sources,
and I find myself again, at peace.

I walk away and I return to myself—
whole, healed, at peace.

May we know peace.
May we seek and find peace.
May we live peace. Amen.

I . . .

I *believe* in God.
    I *believe* that all life and living, is Sacred.
        I *believe* that the Light of God is within us all—
            deep within us all.
                I *base* my life and my actions and my faith,
                    on these truths.

I *trust* in God. Implicitly.
    I *trust* in myself.
        And I *strive* to trust more and more in humanity,
            despite my present living in a scary, changing world,
                built on the ideals
                    of some greedy, power-hungry mortals.

I *hope* for many things in this world, and in my life.
    Balance. Equilibrium. Equality.
        Peace. Understanding, Compassion. Respect. Justice.
            Love.
                Most of all, I *hope* for universal, unbridled,
                    unconditional love, among all.

I *know* who I am, and I *delight* in being me.
    No doubts. No second thoughts. No regrets. No reserve.
        I *know* that I have been given many gifts—
            I *know* that I've have been bestowed many blessings.
                I *know* in my heart what is good and right,
                    and most often, true. I *know* my God.

I *am* strong. I *am* vital. I *am* worthy.
I *am* meant to be here,
learning, growing, becoming, transcending.
I *am* meant to share, abundantly.
I, *am* loved.

I *can* set goals. I *can* take action. I *can* use my voice.
I *can* share my gifts. I *can* begin. I *can* make a difference.
I *can*, and I *will.*

I *am* healed of all that which once upon a time broke me.
I *put* all of my shattered pieces back together
with a new and trusty glue.
My wounds have left scars but in the whole picture—
in my eyes—they are just that—
only that—simply scars.
They do not define me.

I *am* whole.
And in my wholeness I *have* integrity.
And in my integrity, I *have* peacefulness.
I *am* at peace.

I *desire* to become more/most fully human,
in all that is me, in all that I do.
I *strive* to become more/most fully human.
I *vow* to become more/most fully human with my
love and compassion leading the way.

I *honor* my God. I *honor* His gifts. I *honor* His love.
I pray that I may serve God with all the gifts I have been given.
I *pray* for the strength and the courage
to rise up to listen for—and to answer to—
God's call on my life.

I *humbly pray* that I may shine, like my father—Buddy.
I *pray* that my God can see the shining.
I *pray* that in God's seeing, God smiles. Amen.

HOLY LIGHT—CURVED LIGHT—LOVELIGHT

I'm all grown up now.
  I know who I am and who I want to be.

I'm not sure where life is heading, but that doesn't matter,
  because I know I'll move forward
    through the storms, up the hills,
      through the murky waters and the swamps—
        I'll move forward with integrity, and with hope, and with passion.
          There will always be
            Light on my path—and Light in my heart.
              Holy Light—Curved Light—Lovelight.

In my retiring years, I am evolving.
  Nevermore will I seek or await another's approval,
    or find myself cowering under their control,
      their contempt, or their disdain.

Never will I ever allow another's negative energy to shape my personhood.
  Never again will I need to measure my worth—
    or even worse—prove my worth.
      Nevermore will I shrink away,
        defeated, demeaned, devalued—
          dehumanized.

I am worthy. I am strong.
  I stand tall against all that threatens
    to cut me, to break me,
      to harm me or haunt me or limit me.

I am loved. Beloved. Befriended.
Cared for. Comforted. Chosen. Called.
Encouraged, and empowered, and enlightened.
I am gathered in. I am groomed. I am graced.
I am held. Held close. Lifted. Lifted up.

The sky is wide, wide, wide open, but the horizon is still quite visible.
I have a place, here, in this vastness.
I have a place, here, in the interconnectedness of all life.
I am grounded. I am able.

Ever and always, in my exquisite spaciousness of being,
"I can put out my hand and touch the face of God."[10]

I am ready to live out my life as a sharing, caring and daring soul—
as an energy and an entity to be reckoned with.
I'm free—I'm set free—so free at last.

I breathe, therefore I live, therefore I live strong—
strong in my self-worth,
strong in my faith,
strong in my *raison d'etre.*

I am Janis. I am me. I am present, here and now.
I am Sacred. I am of the Light. I am Light.
I move forward. In the Light. Forever in the Light.
In this, there is no darkness, only Light.

There will be storms—tornadoes and tsunamis.
There will be powers and controls, beyond my control.
And of course, there will be negativity—
and power-hungry-mean-spiritedness-
and-thoughtless-selfishness too.

10. John Gillespie Magee, "High Flight" in *Pittsburgh Post-Gazette Newspaper, November 12, 1941.*

Here, in my retiring years,
I have truly had the time to rediscover me, *the real me—*
the one that got buried under years of self-neglect in the career world—
the one that emerged through darkness into the Light.
I am returning to me.
I am re-valuing me.
I am seeing me anew—with fresh eyes and vision.

And, the Light is ever with me.
Curved Light—Lovelight—
a Holy Light that curves
into all the nooks and crannies and corners, of me.
Curved Light—Lovelight, is my strength, my matrix,
my essence, my soul.
Curved Light—Lovelight—
illuminates my soulscape.
Thanks be. Amen.

CLOSING PRAYER

STORY, COMMENTARY, AND AFFIRMATION—
All in a Prayer of Gratitude

Dear Father God—God of Mystery—God of Light.
  Dear God of Holy Lovelight, please hear my prayer.

All life changes, evolves, emerges, transforms, transcends—
  through the tick and the tock of the travels of time.
    I learn. I grow. I become.
      I strive. I thrive.
        I shape. I shade. I shine.
          All in your grace.
            All in your presence.
              All in your time.

I live in a world that is innately interconnected.
  My broad reach and my subtle influence,
    they both speak to the powers of my relational living,
      to my communal ways,
        and to my wholesome interdependence.
          They speak to the Servant Heart in me,
            and to the Compassionate Life
              I choose to lead.

But it is you God, who sustains me.
  I live in your created world as a steward of the earth.

It is my very relationship with you
  that grounds me and stills me—that leads me on in the Light.

With you, I am living in the Light.
Living loud in the Light!
With you, I am known, loved and understood.
With you, I am becoming
the Child of God—the Child of Light—
that you have called me to be.

You God, are the artist—the artist of my soul.
More than the potter's hand.
More than the maestro or choir conductor.
You are the artist of my soulscape—
the watercolor painter
of my blotted, bleeding, billowing soulscape.
You formed me.
You are still forming me, here and now.

And in these words, I rest.
It is in this understanding that I find
comfort, contentment, and peace.

It is in you, through you, and with you,
that I come into
exquisite self knowledge, self understanding,
and self awareness.

The depth of my colorfully textured soulscape
is ever emerging in the dawning Holy Lovelight.
My essence and my very being are shining brightly,
by your artful hands.

I now, am Light.
My soulscape shimmers in gratitude for you.

Yours is a love that knows no limits.
Yours is a grace beyond understanding.
Yours in me, is a work
of pure poesy, pure presence and provision,
would I ever and always
open myself to your doing—
open myself to the works of your hands.

I give thanks for you, my heavenly Father.
And, I give special thanks for Buddy, my earthly father.
I am strong. I am whole. I have integrity. I am loved.

I am empowered to live in the Light, through both of you—
through the artists' tender and loving hands.
Through both of you,
my *Soulscape* is alive—in the Light. Amen.

OTHER BOOKS BY THE AUTHOR

1. *Random and Nebulous—Nuancing the Psalms*, Wipf and Stock, Eugene, OR, 2021
2. *Light Beyond the River*, Wipf and Stock, Eugene, OR, 2022
3. *My Indulgent Interior Life*, Wipf and Stock, Eugene, OR, 2023
4. *Wholehearted Me—A-Z!*, Wipf and Stock, Eugene, OR, 2024
5. *Zahryn's Light—Across the Waters*, Wipf and Stock, Eugene, OR, 2025

For more details, please visit
Janis Constable's author website at

www.janisconstablebooks.com

BIBLIOGRAPHY

Brontë, Charlotte. *Jane Eyre*. London: Smith, Elder and Co., 1847.

Eliot, T. S. "Little Gidding." In *Four Quartets*. London: Faber and Faber, 1943.

Frost, Robert. "Stopping by Woods on a Snowy Evening." In *New Hampshire*. New York: Henry Holt, 1923.

Keats, John. "Ode on a Grecian Urn." In *Annals of Fine Arts for 1820 Volume 5*. London: Sherwood Neely and Jones, 1820.

Magee, John Gillespie. "High Flight." *Pittsburgh Post-Gazette*, November 12, 1941.

Tennyson, Alfred. "Ulysses." In *Poems by Alfred Tennyson in Two Volumes*. London: Edward Moxon, 1842.

Thoreau, Henry David. *Walden*. Boston: Ticknor and Fields, 1854.

Whittier, John Greenleaf. "The Brewing of Soma." *The Atlantic Monthly*, April 1872.

Wordsworth, William. "Tables Turned." In *Lyrical Ballads*. London: J. and A. Arch, 1798.

Yeats, William Butler. "Down by the Salley Gardens." In *The Wanderings of Oisin and Other Poems*. London: Kegan Paul Trench, 1889.

www.ingramcontent.com/pod-product-compliance
Lightning Source LLC
LaVergne TN
LVHW050631100826
845148LV00011B/1822

* 9 7 9 8 3 8 5 2 6 2 9 4 6 *